UNHEARD OF:

I VOW TO NEVER BE SILENT

By
Cassandra Edouard

Copyright 2022 ©

Unless otherwise identified, Scripture quotations are taken from the following Bible versions, Scripture quotations are from the World English Bible (WEB) and King James Version Bible (KJV) Used by permission. All rights reserved.

DISCLAIMER

The advice contained in this material might not be suitable for everyone. The author designed the information to present her opinion about the subject matter. The reader must carefully investigate all aspects of any business decision before committing to him or herself. The author obtained the information contained herein from sources she believes to be reliable and from her own personal experience, but she neither implies nor intends any guarantee of accuracy. The author is not in the business of giving legal, accounting, or any other type of professional advice. Should the reader need such advice, he or she must seek services from a competent professional. The author particularly disclaims any liability, loss, or risk taken by individuals who directly or indirectly act on the information contained herein. The author believes the advice presented here is sound, but readers cannot hold her responsible for either the actions they take or the risk taken by individuals who directly or indirectly act on the information contained herein.

Published by 2Kings Publishing Company, LLC
Printed in the United States
Copyright © 2022 by Cassandra Edouard
ISBN 979-8-218-10280-7

Powerful Quotes from an Inspirational and Spiritual Teacher:

"When you stand and share your story in an empowering way, your story will heal you and your story will heal somebody else."
— Iyanla Vanzant

"You can accept or reject the way you are treated by other people, but until you heal the wounds of your past, you will continue to bleed. You can bandage the bleeding with food, with alcohol, with drugs, with work, with cigarettes, with sex, but eventually, it will all ooze through and stain your life. You must find the strength to open the wounds, stick your hands inside, pull out the core of the pain that is holding you in your past, the memories, and make peace with them."
— Iyanla Vanzant

"Everything that happens to you is a reflection of what you believe about yourself. We cannot outperform our level of self-esteem. We cannot draw to ourselves more than we think we are worth."
— Iyanla Vanzant

"Fear wears so many clever disguises it is virtually impossible to always recognize it. Fear disguises itself as the need to be somewhere else, doing something else, not knowing how to do something or not needing to do something."
— Iyanla Vanzant

(https://www.goodreads.com/author/quotes/15508.Iyanla_Vanzant)

Table of Contents

Introduction 1

Preface 3

Deceptive 6

Vengeance Is Mine "Bitter Ole Me" 16

Her Confession (Part 1) 30

Detoxified My Soul Prayer 40

The Power In Self-Investment, Women 52

Men-Drunk-En-Ness (His Story) 79

Conversation of Confessions (Part 2) 87

Man's Self-Esteem 90

The Planet of A Foolish Woman 98

I Have A Voice Too 101

Gem 101: The Lesson 104

The Planet of A Wise Wo-Man 107

Fear of Rejection 119

Perception: Me, Myself, And Them 132

Identity Stolen 140

Yield Ladies 143

Present Self 171

The Voice 174

Love: Forgiveness, Reconnecting, Restoring 178

No More 183

Acknowledgments 195

INTRODUCTION

This book was written from a place of numbness, hurt, and pain which unlocked doors to unhealed wounds. My past traumas caused me to live in bondage, fear, and repeated cycling pain. I was self-inflicted, afflicted and confused, while suffering silently. I felt no one understood my pain and would view me differently. I needed inner healing, soul-surgery, peace, strength, and love. So, I am dedicating this book, mainly to those individuals who have suffered silently from their untold stories. In other words, those who have been silenced by relationship trauma, childhood trauma, urban trauma, identity crises, low self-esteem, suicidal thoughts, depression and anxiety, self-love, and cycling pain (hurt people hurt people). Those who felt they had no one to share their pain with due to fear of judgment, shame, and guilt. Those living in mental bondage, confusion, and self-infliction, who felt misunderstood, isolated, and rejected. And for those whose pride, and ego have hindered their self- growth. All these underlying negativities have re-created new identities for us in redefining, shaping, expressing, and accepting who we are and who we aspire to be. However, as you read through this book, I hope you are inspired and find courage to heal. For this is a self-guided educational book and for some a motivational and inspirational book.

As you read further, you will see that each chapter in this book has its own unique story. And I believe this book will be a voice to the voiceless, give peace to the hopeless, clarity, and the willpower to move forward. In some degree or another, we may relate or know someone who will. Finally, as a human, we should never judge a person by his or her circumstances, because you never know why or how. Everyone does not have the willpower as you, not everyone know how to move forward when they feel restricted or limited, tie down due to circumstances. And you will never know when you will face similar life challenges. Depression is real, life trauma is real especially when people are going through life experiences alone. No matter who you are, what position you hold, what title you have, or what volume your character speaks, we should never judge.

If you have overcome these challenges, do not stick your nose at that person, thinking you are better. Better yet, even if you did not walk in their shoes; pray with them, guide them in the right direction of seeking help, motivate them, HELP them if you can, and or, say a prayer for them. The reality of it is that we just need someone to give us a helping hand, share their story, or just support us, and showing up can make a difference. Let us not judge and be the voice to help others break free from their trauma, and their untold stories so that we all can be free. In good faith, I stand with you in finding the help that you need, from your past, to stop recreating cycling pain.

PREFACE

Although some parts of this novel are based on a real-life event. Any resemblances to actual events, real people, living, organizations, establishments, or locales are products of the author's imagination. Other names, characters, places, and incidents are used fictionally. Everything mentioned is based on personal knowledge and experience. This book is not intended for my readers to attack anyone or any organizations, but to simply help, bring awareness, and educate the effects of keeping silent.

It started when I became silenced by my untold stories. I became silenced by fear, silenced by guilt, silenced within, and silenced by him. It put me at a dark place in my life - where I did not know who I was and who I wanted to be. More significantly, I became afflicted by my past. It created mixed emotions for me. I was so hurt that it created new identities for me. Unconsciously I put myself on a psychological and emotional roller coaster. Living life in spiritual stagnation caused my emotions to be driven on autopilot. I was allowing my past and the little voices in my head to dictate for me. Believing everything that was lingering in my head to be true. Then it shifted gear. I crashed — ended in a danger zone.

Dangerously enough to put me back in a dark space emotionally, spiritually, psychologically, and physically, and had me thinking people were against me, living in my truth, going in circles, and crying, why me? Continuously, I lived in bondage, with damaged emotions, and in total confusion. Doing and saying things based on my emotions. Repeating the same old pattern of "hurt people hurt people" and playing and creating victim(s) of myself. Then I found myself unintentionally recreating a sequence of pain, based on my past trauma and self-rejections. I made people pay for my past and actions and destroyed the little chance I had at happiness. I then became resentful. Trusting no one -made it hard for me to be free because I felt those who loved me did not have my best interest at heart. Little did I know my mind was playing tricks with me and making me think everyone was against me because I was operating under self-inflicted limitations. I literally felt alone, with no one to turn to.

Yet, I was depressed and wished I should have ended my life too. Living in silence and not letting anyone know my pain. I felt safe there, being in my dark place. I wished I had someone genuine enough to talk to who was trustworthy, wouldn't judge, and was willing to speak life back to me. I wanted this feeling of depression to go away. Slowly but shortly, I started losing everything and everyone around me. I became desperate for some positive change. Praying to God for inner healing and seeking help, I became desperate. I realized I had so much to offer and so much to give. So, I could not allow myself to go down that dark path. I decided to seek help. I enrolled myself in Christian counseling, continue to attend church, and listen to motivational and inspirational leaders.

As I am continuing my healing journey. I needed inner healing, spiritual growth, spiritual covering, guidance, increasing in my faith, and a closer relationship with God. Lastly, I try my best to apply and practice biblical principles and standards; also sow uncommon seed – an uncomfortable seed for my breakthrough (to overcome my life challenges and trauma and to see my future harvest). I have invested in my life for inner healing and to manifest what I desire. When sowing seed, you have to make sure the ground you sow into is fertile- bear fruit and you are led by God to sow. That's another conversation. Sowing is truly important when you know the ground you are sowing into. It is the same as receiving a prophecy. Be careful with that.

After reading this book, I pray you vow to never be silence again, never be hurt again, and no more of whatever the "it" maybe in your life. I pray your self-confidence increases and improve in the area's needed. I urge you to pray, seeking God for counsel, healing, peace, and strength. I hope for you to be in a space of replenishing for a healthy new beginning. I hope you wouldn't repeat the cycle of hurt and pain that you have suffered, inwardly and outwardly. I hope you would accept, acknowledge, change, and forgive yourself and other people who have hurt you. Lastly, I hope for you to face your past to gain full access to SELF again. For I do not have the answers to all problems that we may face. However, I hope you know that you are not alone. If you are willing to let God, he has all the answers. I would like to share a quote from the book called, *Why Women Act Foolish*, by Dr. Veronica G. Bee. She stated, "Hurt people hurt people, but healed people heal people." I pray this book heals you so you can heal someone else.

DECEPTIVE

Deceptive: is tending or having the power to cause someone to accept as true or valid what is false or invalid: tending or having the power to deceive. (https://www.merriam-webster.com/)

Myra was beautiful, intelligent, and creative. A strong-minded individual who didn't allow anyone's opinion to factor into hers. She was the type that walked around with her crown held up high—a big heart, and a big smile. Nothing bothered her. She was a hard-shelled woman with no cares in the world. She was the ideal strong woman a man would consider. She knew how to hold it together. She was the role model that everyone looked up to, a passionate speaker, and very persuasive and wise. Her advice was just motivating, pure, and on point. She had that voice that no man or woman could touch. Her vibe and spirit were just one of a kind—the type of person you would want to be around. Her smile alone changed your negative vibe. But sometimes, she wished she knew how to kill the noisome voices in her head, well the negative ones. She wished the same advice and motivations she gave to encourage others; could have been applied to herself. However, that was not her case.

Honestly, how many of us practice what we preach? We are so quick to play the role of authentic, but behind closed doors, we are as fake as a disposable plate. We are not true to ourselves until we unmask who we truly are. Even then, we still live a lie because we cannot face the reality. We cannot accept who we truly are because we lost our sense of self; our identity. Well, she had. She was the definition of someone else's fantasy. Myra had a platform, but lost herself in the moment of time, living a life trying to please people until reality hit. Life came at her. It came at her so fast that, unconsciously, it led her into depression. Now she was dealing with lots of anxiety. Depression became her best friend. No one knew what she was thinking because she disguised it with attractive lies and a big smile. Hiding behind her truth, she had been making herself believe that everything was just fine. Dealing with childhood trauma, self-afflictions, pride, and self-imagery, she always felt defeated. Beneath it all, she was dying inside, but it was just a matter of time before she released those sleeping demons inside her. That was when she learned about her true self—in the midst of her afflictions.

We probably have that one girlfriend that is deceptive about life. Living a lifestyle that is not defined by hers. Living that grandiose life, chasing perfection and materialistic things, and having men thinking she is that thang. Presenting this so-called reality that is unrealistic and untrue, convincing others she is living her best life too. Flaunting on Instagram, Twitter, Facebook, and YouTube. You name it, she is famous. Being excessively proud and the fake life she represented, she is too afraid to admit to others that she too, is struggling, and dealing with her self-afflictions. She is living under the roof of someone else's rentals, calling it the luxurious life, and popping expensive wine, but her bank account says otherwise. Living above her means, she creates comfortability. She is not happy with where she is in life but carries herself with hidden agendas and camouflaged high standards.

She continues to pursue living based on her set expectations. Portrays to have it all together, chasing the finer things in life, but filled with looming emotional hurts and gradually dying inside. At any given moment, suicide is her way out. Life is not how she expected it to be. Debts after debts, crisis after crisis, she continues putting herself in deeper holes but managing to find her way out just to keep up the life she faked. As far as her love life, well, she is cold-hearted and had been that way for a while, living by the motto "I will rather be safe than sorry," meaning before a man can break her heart, she will break his. Her personality was just enough to suck you in. She would use men for what they had to benefit her pockets and keep her satisfied. Instead of working on herself and her past baggage, she brought that negativity into her new relationship.

Dupris was 6 ft, light skin, hazel nut eyes and curly short hair. He was built like an athletic, played basketball, charming, and sweet as a rose. Dupris was an assistant basketball coach for the college team, the owner of the trucking company Dalless Inc, and the CEO/promoter of club Flex. He was the type to make his presence known even during your hard times to show you that you are not alone. He was everything a woman dreamed of in a man. The man that would hold your hands in private and in public, take long walks on the beach, cuddle, show you off to the world, and is affectionate in his gestures to you. He would call you just to say I love you, send you weekly flowers, and would make it his business to fix you a hot plate. When you are sick, he knew the right remedy to make you whole. The man that would leave a woman speechless with no worries in the world. He cared for her, went out his way for her, paid her bills, cooked and cleaned. Dupris brought her pads, paid for random vacations, surprised her with romantic dinners, and ran her bubble baths. He even took care of her car mechanics and gave her special massages. He loved her as his reflection. He was just that man. He was the hashtag—example of relationship goal or hashtag—example of a real man. Dupris was the guy with the corny jokes who made you laugh and smile, often uncontrollably. She started to feel his love was too good to be true. She questioned, "How can a man love someone like me?" Her negative thoughts started creeping in, covering a large distance with every subtle step and now she was afflicted, confused, and slipping back to her old ways and living by the motto, "I will rather be safe than sorry." What he did not know was that she had a quantum of negative memories and was dealing with her insecurities, her damaged past, and her self-affliction. It was like she had one foot in and one foot out, unsure of what the outcome of the relationship would be because the results were now too good to be true. She became consumed by her thoughts and started mishandling him due to being scared to love and past triggers. Love became too much of a demand because she did not know what love really meant. She started to share too much of her past which had him wondering if she had a hidden agenda. She talked about her abortions, being rejected and having low self-esteem, dealing with depression and suicidal thoughts. She mentioned being cheating on and cheating one of her ex, dealing with dudes for their money, breaking men hearts after six months into the relationships, and how she had one of her dudes give her a sexual massage while talking on the phone with her man. All the stuff she should have kept to herself or spoke to therapist about. All she wanted to do was release the skeletons in her closet and take a chance at healing. He could not handle it, so he started gaslighting her, manipulating her and making her feel worthless; shaming and blaming her. He started to feel that she was not giving him the attention that he needed nor giving him her true authentic self. Therefore, the relationship took a negative turn, she begins to believe in his manipulating words and started acting and moving differently and he started to see a different side of her. She began to push him off because he questioned her sanity. He created confusion in her life- thinking she was the problem when the real problem was him; he was hurt and scared, his past started to creep up on him and started to reveal his hidden pain. Even in the midst, he continued to be good at loving but only to his measures. They began blaming each other, playing games, and then, the secret cheating began.

They became less attractive to each other, annoyed with each other's presence, and communication started to fall off. The relationship began spiraling and his words started to affect her performance as a woman even when she desired to do better. Negative thoughts started presenting themselves to her due to the fear of rejection. At times, she would give up on the relationship, feeling hopeless, and unworthy. She started to not give a fuck or make any effort to make the relationship work or last. The relationship started to fail with its jar of life dripping into emptiness which pushed him even more toward other women. Stress started taking over them, and negative thoughts and energy continue to follow them. Their love became toxic, words became weapons, and actions became violent. They verbally, physically, and emotionally abuse each other, using each other past as a tool to gain one up on each other. Telling each other they are a mistake, and they regret pursuing this relationship.

He started feeling everything he had invested into this relationship was taken for granted, feeling faded, the love was lost and gone, and the flowers in the garden of love were all dried out. Things became questionable. He started to lose himself; he felt played, unworthy, unwanted, unloved, trust was gone, and less of the man he have become; actually, at this point, he was. He started blaming her for his wrongdoings and projecting his wrongdoings onto her just to silence her. His false thinking created trust issues; their past events became the highlight of their relationship. They both played the mastermind game of controlling and manipulating each other, leading each other down a toxic road. So, everything they worked hard for went down the drain. He departed and she was left naked, broken, shattered, and feeling worthless again.

In a way, everyone knew their relationship was not in great standing, but she kept making excuses to make it looks good. The relationship was so toxic that it opened doors for other women, who were snaking in the garden ready to bite and destroy the helplessly dying flowers of what remained of their love. Opportunity started presenting itself, so he started to sway astray. Other women started whispering and planting seeds in his head, feeding his ego. He started gravitating towards them, selling his soul for attention because they were attractive and selling him fake lofty dreams. He felt they were the real deal because he had a taste of their world. Distracting him from going back to her. They were luring him in like the snake they were, to trap him into their whims and caprices, making him sexually deranged, so he can be their prize possession. When he did return, he would say how much he loved her and wanted them to work things out for the better- but gone missing for weeks at a time, just to get a call, saying sorry bae, I'm working late, or need time alone. When he is drunk, the real come out. They say out of the heart speaks, he calls her all kinds of names. She felt so confused, particularly as to why this was happening to her, and why she could not handle him. She tried to get him back, but his lust was too deep in them.

She was a fool for thinking everything was sweet too, feeding into his bullshit while he was feeding other women bigger shit. He was lost in his drama, playing the lead role of confusion and self-confliction. There was a fake love that she did not recognize until he was slipping away, and she started exposing his dark secrets. He became a cheater and started resenting her. Their relationship took a shift to more toxicity. The home was not his own. Late nights became his mornings, and his mornings became his late nights. His focus was on the other women who gave him great nights. What he was craving was great intimacy, great talks, and attention from anyone vulnerable to cater to his needs. He only went home for a little satisfaction and a cooked meal. His honesty made her thought she had it made. He made her feel wanted, but in secrecy, his mind was already made.

The patterns of his behaviors of coming home late, ignoring phone calls, and not eating home-cooked meals repeated more and more and he spent less time at home. She started to notice his patterns, yet she remained. She wanted real love, the love she experienced in the past with him. She continued to be led by his foolish lies and the deceitful kisses. Lies after lies, she still yearn for his love. Tears after tears she pleaded and begged for him to stay home and to love her the same way as he once did. Dupris couldn't help but wanted to have his cake and eat too. So, he played the role of a forgiver and made her think everything with her was great. Yet, he was receiving phone calls and text messages from different women, at all kinds of hours saying, "I love you," "I miss you," "I haven't seen you, come home." Although disrespect followed disrespect, she remained silent to the hurt and pain.

She did not even have a mind of her own. After several late-night cries. Myra felt terrified, terrified at the fact that she did not have a voice, sufficient courage, or a backbone to stand up for herself. She was so choked up in her emotions that words could not express how she felt. She was drowning and did not have the willpower to swim through her emotional ocean. She only wished God would take her life. She was no longer herself. She became his puppet, his property, and his mockery. His insecurities created challenges, problems, false and negative thinking, and a lack of trust. He was just bitter, nasty, and angry at the world. He was in bondage and wanted to trap her in it, too. She knew but was afraid to speak up because she was blinded by love. Foolish by the thought or afraid of losing him. Why is love so blind and foolish? She questioned herself. She hated herself for believing that things would work out between them; but to be honest, the backbone to do the right thing was shattered. She ignored all her exes' knowing that one of them was dying to keep her and make her his wife.

The relationship became more toxic and damaging, still claiming this man, while he is entertaining other women, taking them out, buying them name-brand bags and clothes, paying for their beauty just to show he is the man- because of the void he was feeling within his own home. To top it all off, she began to relive the trauma from past relationships. Playing in her head the embarrassment of "everyone knew their business." While she carried her crown, it kept tilting with no one to fix it or readjust it. So, she stayed quiet and stayed in her lane- minding her own business, watching everything she worked hard for play out and crumble down at her feet. Anxiety kicked in, and she became stressed and depressed thinking about all the things she experienced from the past years of her life. Even the hidden things she did not talk about. She was in her mind ready to explode. She was bottling in all hurt and pain. Her little enemy kept telling her, "You should take your life and not deal with none of this sh*t called life."

And yes, silence kills. It's a deadly weapon that empowers every negative emotion asleep within us. It becomes lethal to the spirit and poison to the soul. She was depressed and no longer herself. She stops loving herself and allowed him to manipulate her, interrogate her, and make excuses to keep using her. How could he treat a woman, whom all she wanted was to be loved, with little or no value? How could he blame her for his mistakes and his insecurities? How could he say I love you when he kept going to his exes for answers? How could he treat another woman better than she or give other women what we used to have? They must have been around the same time she was for him to have moved on so quickly the way he did. In her mind, if she or they satisfied you better than I did, why do you keep coming back? She was pondering what was she giving you that I was not. Her silent tears had her choked up. She couldn't express herself because she was hurt. She would cry herself to sleep, asking God why her? She was trying to numb this pain while still burying past hurt and pain. How did silence kill? There was no hope for the future because all she saw was a failed relationship. In her thoughts: All I saw, breathed, and heard was negativity. Every response was negative. Now, he was leaving me naked with no food to eat. Trust had left the scene. Here I was picking up the pieces along with taking care of his shit and while getting myself together. So now, I was laying down at night, crying my eyes out, not knowing where to start and how to begin, trying to live by faith and not by sight. Then I start to think about how life could be, how he could turn his back on me, not just once, but multiple times. Here comes the inner voices, depression opened the door, and everything around me began to eliminate itself from my list. I was left with just suicide.

Acting as a strong woman but weak inside, she lost a part of herself, her identity, her womanhood; she betrayed herself. She became her worst enemy. She wished love did not call her home. She told herself, "Don't be fooled by the sweet talks and sweet kisses." It was all a manipulation. Unfortunately, to others he was the public figure, making people believe he was all that for her. Dupris made her feel less of a woman, downplayed her, degraded her, and took away her pride. He questioned, how could her love, be so dangerous. He tore her down and stripped her naked and took away her discretion to consent. Sex became emotionless, and to him, she was copper. She was not as pure as gold because once in a blue moon, she became rusty. Myra was no longer authentic because she did not know who she was, only who she should be. She became numb, desensitized to the world because the world had nothing to offer. She started accepting his wrongs, his nakedness, and his drunkenness. She had no voice to explain what transpired in the wall of her relationship because with a smile, she had shown what is. So, she remained silent, silent within, and silent to him.

Disclaimer for the next chapter: Before, I knew the difference between karma and reap what you sow. I believed karma and reaped what you sow meant the same. Until I did research and found there is a difference. I chose this definition from an online blog by Britnee Bradshaw for a better breakdown. According to Britnee Bradshaw (2022), "On a surface level perspective, karma bridges the gap between good actions (or intentions) and good results as well as bad actions (or intentions) and bad results. Essentially, what a person reaps in this life can be a consequence of what they sowed in their previous lives. What a person sows now, they will reap in future life. And karma can accumulate, giving you a chance to balance out positive or negative consequences."

(Bradshaw, Britnee. January 17, 2022. https://www.ibelieve.com/faith/what-is-the-difference-between-karma-and-reaping-what-you-sow.html).

VENGEANCE IS MINE "BITTER OLE ME"

"Honestly, karma, you take too long to do your job. I want revenge and I want it now! I am hurting, can't you see? I have been losing sleep when I am supposed to be stress-free. I should not have been worrying about someone who had done me wrong. Why are you taking so long? Do you not see or feel my pain? Do you not hear my cry? Why haven't you responded yet? Take action NOW! Well, since you can't do the job, I'll take care of it myself."

- Cassandra Edouard

I hate when you call a guy, and he doesn't answer or places you on the block list. So, I pop up at his side chick house playing Jazmine Sullivan song, "I bust the windows out your car." Yes, his beautiful red Telsa and now her white Saturn Sky. Screaming meet me outside. Okay, I lied. But I sure did set them up. He always talked about having a threesome. So, I'd called the girl and we made plans. We created this whole story line of how we are going to give him the night of his life. This chick ! As I said to myself, rolling my eyes. We linked up, off course. And it sure went down, right at the hotel. The set up was nice, we showed up in our lingerie and the jacuzzi running with bubbles. As he walked through the door, R.Kelly was playing, seem's like you're ready. (Yeah, ready to die). She blindfolded him and I pushed him onto the bed. We tied him up, then BOOM!!! That's where the drama began. As she was seducing him and getting him arouse, I put on my brass knuckles, and I knocked her out. Then I punch his elephant trunk so hard, his urethra split apart. Maybe he will learn this time around, not to play with my emotions.

Yeah, I get crazy! And it felt good doing it. I felt like a champion, walked out like yeah hoe, I bet you won't ever take my man again. I got in my car and blast the song; I get crazy by Nicki Minaj (2009). When I reached the red light, the song Be careful with me by Cardi B (2018) started playing. Girl, I sung my heart out. I am not even hood, but I was that night. By the time, I reached home, I had Ciara (2015) playing on repeat, "I bet your start loving me, soon as I start loving someone else. Somebody better than you. I bet you start needing me. Soon as you see me with someone else somebody other than you", singing while tears rolling down my face. I walked inside the house, took my shoes off, poured me a glass of wine and drown in depression. I started thinking about all the memories we shared and things that could have been, while singing Beyonce, I got Me, Myself and I."

Dang, that hotel drama was wild. I'm sorry things got out of hand, but the whole time, I was creating that story line in my little ole head. As I was envisioning, how I wanted to murder, the both of them. The more I replayed the scenario, the more hurt and angrier I became. All these negative thoughts had me bitter and triggered. As much as I wanted it to go down, I had too much to lose and too much to risk. Why does my heart bleed over a man that does not love or appreciate me? Love me the way I deserved to be loved. Hides me in public but behind closed doors, he treats me like his queen to be. Acknowledge me through text messages and phone calls but cannot acknowledge my presence in front of his friends, family, and all. My heart is so broken, badly bruise by blinded love. Hurt to the point, I want you to feel how painful my heart is in. And if karma doesn't hit you the way you emotionally hit me. I hope it hit someone close to you so you can see while they experience a broken heart. I have heard what a person sows they shall reap, what goes around comes around, and everything that happens in the dark must come to light. So, do not worry, it will come back to you. As I drowned in depression and isolate myself from everyone, even the world. I'll be praying that karma gives you a special visitation for all the wrong you have done to me.

My prayer:

I hope he feels every bit of the pain I felt. I hope he experiences the lonely nights, teary eyes, and a shattered heart. I hope the women uses him and take advantage of everything he has. Break his little ole heart and throw him in the trash or feed him to the hyenas. They'll enjoy him! I hope the women turn against him the way he turned against me. I hope they go crazy and make him wish the grass wasn't greener on the other side. I hope his spirit torments him for leaving me to entertain these women. I hope he calls my name in his sleep while lying next to them or while he is diving deep inside of them. I hope he dreams of me sexing another man and wakes up upset because it felt so real. I hope we cross paths and sees me flirting with another man. And to the main side chick, hmm… Well, I hope she walks out on you and play you like a fool. I hope she keeps stalking you until she drives you wild. I hope she hits your finances, and you lose it all. Your house, your car, your job, and even your mind. Yes! That mind of yours. So, when you come back, you have nothing but my a** to kiss. I want you to feel desperate like I did. Depressed and all. I hope. I just hope, you reap what you have sown.

They say hurt people hurt people. And unfortunately, I want revenge. They say Karma is a B****? So, the question remains, "when will they suffer from what they did? Do you understand the sensation of a razor blade cutting through your heart as you sit and wonder, "What the hell did I do wrong to deserve this?" Wondering, when will this turmoil go away? Trauma after trauma, pain after pain. The more, I revisit the hidden past, the more damage it brings. The tears, the heartbreaks, the betrayals, the infidelity, the let downs. So much has been done to me. I became bitter that I could not see the best for me. I felt everything around me falling apart, coming in full circle to tear me apart. Reminding me of my unhealed scars. The scares that will forever leave a mark. Maybe a lasting imprint on my memory then triggers my heart. The replays of what have had taken place. Pondering and crying asking for this pain to please go away. Silently praying to God for peace. The same peace I had before he came inside of me to destroy my character, my mind, my emotions, my body, and my soul.

As imperfect as I am, the best thing for me to do, is to learn to release and acknowledge what I am feeling, change it by taking back my willpower, and heal by moving forward and not going back to what have hurt me. And ultimately, to let go and let God. Trusting he will mend (heal) my broken-hearted. Praying to learn to manage my emotions, so I don't get easily triggered. I just pray that someone else doesn't trigger this pain. I don't want to put a wall up and cause someone else pain. I pray that I don't hurt again.

Dear Father,

Grant me the serenity to accept what has taken place as a lesson and a blessing. First, I want to say, I am sorry for what I have said earlier. I should not have prayed that witchcraft prayer, that hurt people hurt people, that revenge. For you said in your word that vengeance is mine saith the Lord, and you will repay (Romans 12 vs 19 KJV). Forgive me for my foolish thoughts and words, I have released. For life and death is in the power of our tongue (Proverbs

18 vs 21 KJV). When we pray certain prayers, they come to us and not to those we pray against. My heart hurt. I am broken. I am human. Lord, take this pain from me. He broke me, shattered my heart into pieces. What now? Lord don't let him get away with this. Hurt people are hurting people and that needs to stop. Because people are becoming cold hearted and leaving people heartbroken. Lord, forgive me, if I have done people wrong. I need peace, a compassionate heart, love, grace, and comfort. Help me to live by the fruit of the spirit, to walk in love, joy, peace, gentleness, self-control, meekness (patience and humility), modesty, goodness, generosity, temperance, and in faith (Galatian 5: 22 -23 KJV). I want to be loved and handle with care, have someone gentle with my heart, kiss me with meaning. Father, make me whole, help me to love myself first, and see my worth. I want to see the beauty within me, the value, and the qualities that I hold. For when the next man, the man you have ordained for me, sees me. He sees favor, for I am worth far more than rubies and more precious than gold. For I have outclass the women and surpasses them all. Because I am a woman of noble character despite my imperfections. I deserved it all and much more. I wish him the best because my life is about to spin for the better. I am about to find my identity and bounce back into loving me. The right way because I owe it to myself. Thank you for hurting me. In that case, I rather you, Father, handle it. Amen!

Have you ever wondered about those who have hurt you or those you have hurt? Or what you do to others will come back to you? As previously stated, karma comes in forms you would never think of. Therefore, treat people how you want to be treated or karma will show up and manifest itself. If you are wondering how? There is also a thing called the generational cycle—what you sow, your child or children, those around you or loved ones will reap.

You may not have known but we are probably reaping our parents' cycling pain, past mistakes or poor choices, or the end results of their past. However, karma likes to recreate itself. We all may have experienced hurt by someone who has been hurt by someone. The statement hurt people hurt people is true. We often time take the hurt that we are experiencing and project it onto others. A bleeding soul can contaminate another soul because they are hurt and not properly healed from their past. Whether they do it intentionally or unintentionally, the stains remain because of WORDS, or actions.

At times, we are looking for closure and we go back to the same hurt to be hurt again. This is called a vicious cycle that keeps repeating itself and it never breaks. I've read the book by Dr. Sandra D. Wilson, *Hurt People Hurt People: Hope and Healing for Yourself and Your Relationships*. I highly recommend this book. She stated, "we all have experience hurt by people who were hurt by hurt people. Whether it was by their actions, words, and attitude that are intentionally or unintentionally, visible or invisible, other perpetrated or self- inflicted, physical or non-physical. At the end, it resulted bloody wounds and unseen soul-scars which can last a lifetime (Wilson. 2015)." At some degree or another, we can agree. Those who experiences hurt carries past pain and plant it everywhere they go. Taking those same seeds that have been deeply rooted within, and out of the heart speaks, hurt and pain. Not knowing the affects it has on those we love and those around us. In the aftermath of trauma, hurt people interpret words and actions in a negative light and start to lash out at others, thinking everything that a person says or do is intentional. As if the person is trying to repeat the same hurt, they endured or experienced.

We must learn not pile up hurt on top of hurt to the point it cripples our mind, our heart, and our spirit. As a result, we hurt ourselves, become deeply depressed, frustrated with people, places, and things. Instead of suppressing and or ignore issues, address the "it". What good does it do us? Beside creating a dark place to be in, trust issues, emotional pain, health issues, mental health issues, illness, and sickness. A weak, fatigue, stressed out, and burned-out spirit and body. The worst feeling is to live in bitterness and rage and try to repay the person for what they did to you in the past or make someone else pay for your past hurt. Some of us have been there, rage because of hurt or speak with rudeness or an attitude, ready to kill. Yes, I thought of a million ways to get away with murder. Yes, I have said words that cut like a deadly sword. I felt like getting revenge on the person who did me wrong. Have you? You were in your head plotting how you are going to get your revenge. Some may say revenge is the best feeling. When it all set and done, no one wins in the end. Yes, it is the worst feeling in the world to be played by someone you loved or cared for or people in general. In the end, it does not benefit anyone.

For this reason, we need to heal and release what is hurting, deal with the root of the problem, and never go back to what hurt you. We can become better at dealing with those pain and coping with them better- if we are willing to learn from the hurt and heal from the pain. At some point, we must realize that we are giving too much power to the situation, and we become emotionally irrational, and it does not help to heal the pain within. When we decide not to give too much power and channel that energy towards something positive or do something productive, you will win over the hurt. You become at ease with yourself when you also give it to God. He promised us in his word, Isaiah 61 vs 3, he will give us "beauty for our ashes (KJV)." He will give us comfort in the time of pain, joy for every tear we cry, peace over confusion and uncertainty, heal our broken hearted, strength when we are weak, courage we lack confidence, hope we lack faith, and grace to release us from bondage, fear, troubled spirit, and everything we have gone through. God will wipe the ashes away and put a headdress on our head, cleans us, renew our minds, gives us a new crown. For he is a God of compassion, love, grace, whatever you want him to be, he is.

My question to you is what work have you done to heal within? Have you ever looked at yourself in the mirror and confronted those past hurt and pain? What emotion or feelings arise, or you live with, such as rejection, betrayal, abandonment, trauma, loneliness, hopeless, hurt, or pain? Are you ready and comfortable to bring closure to those wounds? Sometimes it is hard not to keep holding on to the hurtful and painful past with the fear of reopening unhealed wounds or the fear of experiencing the realness, the rawness of the pain. It may be difficult for some to confront without knowing the long-lasting effect it will have on us (because you are still fragile to the situation). So, out of fear, we remain in those emotions and guard our heart where we make it difficult for individuals to love us. We cannot become upset with the ones we pushed away or needed the most because of our self-destructive behavior. Because of this people respond, behave, or react to the way we respond, act or behave.

You become exposed to more trauma which created an identity crisis – a cry for help. Now you are hurt- bleeding on the ones you love whether intentional or unintentionally. Now we both bleeding, spreading our infections amongst innocent souls. Looking for someone to rescue you, heal you, and put a bandage on the affected womb. At the same time, you convince yourself you can do bad all by yourself. F*** the world and everyone in it because it's me against the world. Now that you are in a relationship both party is bleeding and **EXPECTING** each other to heal each other's womb. Neither of you knows how. The deeper you guys get involved, the more wombed you become. You feel the only way out is to continue to bleed on others. Alana Palm stated in her article, *"Hurt People Hurt People: People Manipulate Out of Brokenness,* "their reactions stem from past experiences that led them to certain beliefs that they accepted as truth. They are just preconceived ideas projected onto others to protect their ego (Palm. 2018.)." What hurt people who manipulate out of brokenness do, say things to individuals that they feel about themselves to make themselves feel better; they would hurt someone else for selfish gain. It becomes an ego thing.

Behind people's action, their emotion and feelings present, and they become insensitive to other's because their emotional pain limits their capacity for empathy and self-awareness. I remember as a little girl, I wanted my parents to feel the pain so they can carter to me, seeking love and wanting to know that they love me. There were times, I would say mean things to them- the things they would say to me to them, so they can feel how bad they hurt me. So, I can get one up on them and then rebel against them. I would also plot on hurting myself just to go to the hospital so I can see the hurt in their eyes or make them feel it was their fault. No, it didn't play out because I didn't have the guts to do so. Sometimes people do things, so they won't get hurt at the end. Again, I'm a perfect example. I'd rather play safe than sorry.

Before you play me, I'm going to play you. I feared of getting played or heartbroken, and or did not want to be heartbroken again. I was in relationships whether friendship or partner where I've met people with good heart and created victims out of them, because I was scared to get hurt. I would hurt them first. Or once a person gets close to me, I back up and do things to make them not want to get close to me because I feared love. I would be in relationships with people, manipulate them, disappear for a couple months, and reappear again. Then leave and come back in a different mindset but same patterning. When you do not know what love is, you will test people to see if they truly care or love you. Or handle you at your worst. Hurt people hurt people, however, they often hurt themselves the more. Other reasonings, hurt people that hurt people don't take accountability for their actions. They often live in the past, they play the role of the victim, carry a suspicious spirit, and can't have a trusting relationship due to their past.

An individual that's been hurt won't admit when they are wrong, they will blame others for their past, present, and future pain. Hurt people don't view themselves as wrong. They are fine with making victims out of individuals and living in denial. They won't change what they've done wrong. They have the mindset of when the world turns its back on them, they turn their back on the world. This is an unhealthy toxic way of thinking. Why would you want to project or inflict your pain onto others, because you're the one hurting? Some may say, they are not aware of it because they are accustomed and numb to the pain and the hurt. But listen, we are not each other's experiment, nor can we control what other's do to us. We are human beings with feelings. We must take account for our child-like ways of old residue from childhood hurt, toxic behavior as self-defense mechanism and heal. It is time to mature so we can live a healthy long life.

Word of wisdom: Many of us are trying to fill a void in our lives. There are many factors involved in this. Some desire love, to be made whole, seeking approval, acceptance, and have a sense of belonging too. For others, it may differ. The reality is, we need to **LOVE** ourselves; we can't find love or receive the love we want or desire, if we don't know what it is ourselves. No one can love you the way you do. We do not need that convenient love; unconditional love is what we need. That real love, but to receive it, we must give ourselves that love. Loving and putting ourselves first, we should never come second, last or be an option. If we are far more than rubies, more precious human being walking, then we do not need to be to value or viewed as less than. Also, we should walk around as high valued women with class and spice. Nothing wrong with being a classy woman, with a taste of your personality. Just know who you are! Men will devalue you because you either allowed it or they view themselves as such. It's time to start healing within.

It's time to be responsible and stop creating victims. We can't feed someone sweetness and then poison them later and blame them for taking it. I was the one, my love was sweet until it became poisoned, poisoned enough that I started to hurt genuine people even loved ones. Conflicted in fantasy when, in reality, I was posing. Posing enough to damage a person's soul. Conflicted about self-destruction because of my past damage to my self-construction. How can this be? Don't get close to me, I'm dangerous. You might not get what you see. Hurting from what others did to me. Not consciously realizing that I am mobile destruction, destroying everybody around me. If you're destroyed, I can't damage you because you already have been damaged, damaged enough that our affliction can't afflict each other. A sweet innocent bystander I was until I was washed up and taken advantage of. Now, my heart is so cold that I can't even detach myself. I created victims trying to prove my innocence but instead, I damaged their souls. I took their love for granted but blamed their actions for my behavior. When you sit back and analyze the situation, your actions created all of this. When will you be accountable for your actions? The reality is some people are not willing to take accountability for their actions or try to recognize them, without blaming someone.

We need to come at peace with who we were instead of thinking someone else will give us that peace. The peace we need is within us. Jumping into relationships thinking this one will make up for the last one, won't do it. All we are doing, is bringing more baggage into a new relationship that our spirit did not unpack from the last one or year's. Now, we look like the baggage claims at the airport, waiting to be picked up. Imagine rolling and walking with all those luggage labeled- hurt, pain, bitterness, stress, self-imagery, self-doubt, depression, abandonment, mistrust, violation of privacy, belittlement, embarrassment, neglection, toxic relationship, low-self-esteem, worthless, hopeless, betrayal, domestic violence, exploitation, prostitutions, rejection and etc. Too much to carry right? How long will you continue suffer in silence? This is the time to do some self-reflection, heal from the effect, and change the "it" within, before you make someone else a part of or your baggage entourage, and a victim to your past. The point is we don't need to compartmentalize our feelings by dressing them up. In doing so, we need to understand the "it", address it, acknowledge it and heal it. Heal from negative feelings by forgiving and letting go what was done to you and move forward. You don't want to give too much energy to a circumstance that can, later, kill you.

DO something and MAKE the CHANGE. Write a book, journal, rap about it, sing about it, dance about it, create poetry, direct a play about it, create art, work out, model, join movement, box, kickbox, create a radio show, podcast it, go live, create meme, or create a movement, organization, a rally gathering others who feel the same. If its detrimental to you, always seek counseling from someone you can relate to and who will guide you through self-healing and or find a good church home to attend to help you heal and be delivered from your past pain.

Word of wisdom: First, we must admit we have issues and acknowledge the pain, issues, and or hurt. I have learned to take responsibility for my actions, for my past, and for those, I have done wrong or used. I played the innocent victim, but it was not right. We all have some baggage or have done wrong, and we need to make peace with those we hurt. I want peace in my life, peace within myself, and to be free from negativity and free from my past. Sometimes, you may not get the closure you need, but finding closure with yourself is all you need. Look in the mirror and see yourself for who you are. At times, our character is ugly. Maybe you're at a place where you just don't care. One day, you will and one day it will all make sense. If it doesn't, then it doesn't. I truly believe it will once you sit with yourself and do some real self-reflection.

If the situation is frustrating you and eating you up inside, pray about it and seek good counsel from the wise. In the, James 1:19-20 KJV says, *"Know this, my beloved brothers: let every person be quick to hear, slow to speak, slow to anger; for the anger of man does not produce the righteousness of God."* Proverbs 15:1 KJV says, *"A soft answer turns away wrath, but a harsh word stirs up anger."* Ephesians 4:29 KJV says, *"Let no corrupting talk come out of your mouths, but only such as is good for building up, as fits the occasion, that it may give grace to those who hear."* Ephesians 4:26 KJV says, *"Be angry and do not sin; do not let the sun go down on your anger."* Luke6:45 KJV says, "The good person out of the good treasure of his heart produces good, and the evil person out of his evil treasure produces evil, for out of the abundance of the heart his mouth speaks." (https://www.biblegateway.com). These scriptures basically are telling us how to manage our mouth and behavior, and the kind of heart we should produce because out of your heart speaks how you truly feel, views the world and circumstance around you. Because these scriptures are practical, we can apply them so it can help change our lives.

HER CONFESSION

(Part 1)

Let me explain:

Growing up, I lived by the motto, "I will rather be safe than sorry" to protect my heart from getting hurt, manipulated, and misused. I rather hurt you before you hurt me. Because I will be damn if a man breaks my heart. That is the worst feeling to experience. Especially, when it is done by someone you love or care for, or by someone you thought you would spend the rest of your time living with.

Another thing about me, I had low self-esteem. I did not love myself enough to know my worth or felt pretty enough to know how valuable I am with all my flaws. If someone were to show me, love, I would not know what that felt like or looked like because I did not love myself. I did not appreciate the skin I was in. I did not see myself as worthy nor loved my self-image because social media made me think otherwise. So, I wanted to be everyone else, except for me.

When we met, I fall in love with you. Everything about you from your physical appearance to your swag. I wanted you but was scared to love you. I wanted to love you, but I kept pushing you away, not knowing whether or not I would hurt you. I pushed you away because I did not love myself enough, but on the merits, I deserve you. I just did not know how to handle all the goodness you gave me. I apologize for sharing so much of me and projecting my affliction onto you because I did not know myself and never made the effort to. I apologize if I was too confused to know what I wanted because I wanted the perfect fantasy for great fame. So, here is my pain. As I let my guard down with tears rolling down my eyes. I am more hurt than derange. The pain that I am feeling I would not want anyone to experience, but this is cliché to say. Who hasn't been hurt to the point they go derange? I guess this is why I can share this pain so someone else who has not, does not slip into this pain and the trauma it brought me. Yeah, I need to heal and if you have experienced this or a similar circumstance, let us heal.

So, let us discuss the pain I am feeling inside… I am so hurt and angry at the fact that I kept loving you the way I did, begging you to forgive me and love me in return. I should have paid attention to the red flags instead I kept overlooking them. The reason I overlooked, I don't know; was it love or low self-esteem? As I continue to dwell in sorrow, I constantly thought about the verbal and emotional abuse I have endured. The lies and the cheating. The "I am here for you when you need me, and I love you" and I stayed- thinking things will change. I stuck around praying and hoping one day God will change our relationship. In the process, I was getting played and played like a fool, used, and even reused. Thinking one day you will love me like you once did. Damn, this hurt knowing that things have changed and will stay that way. I am trying to process this situation through, accepting the unexpected is what I tell myself. As I pour my heart into sentences, I am reflecting on the time, I made excuses for your actions. When I would argue with people convincing them your love was different because you express it differently. I asked people to have faith in you because it will be okay. Was that love or was I confused? See, Eve was right, love is blind. Blind enough to keep you in bondage, broken, and damaged. I questioned myself, what is love? Love does not hurt, love values, love is loyal, love is royal, and love is as sweet as it sounds. Damn what was it? Was it the sex? Was I vulnerable? Was I in love? What was it?

Subconsciously, I was hurting myself because I was not like the women that attracted him on social media, thick with small waists and big butts, posing half-naked. Maybe, I was not the kind of girl you were attracted to or would want to hold onto. Maybe I didn't appeal enough to your liking. Those kisses were so fake, that I would accept them anyways. I felt you enjoyed seeing me in pain because you were/are hurt. So, I ask myself, what was it?

Was it your physical attraction? Was it your flaws? As I scroll on Instagram, and look at the idea of happy couples, going on vacations, showing they are in love, and getting married with the perfect family picture. Just laughing with joy in their heart as they promote it to be. Telling myself this is me or this is what I want it to be for myself. Asking myself when this will happen to me. When will I fall in love with the right person that sees me and only me? When will I fall in love with the right person that will love all of me? I guess, I failed myself. Was I not enough for you?

My emotion is involved. I thought we had a connection, and that is what kept me coming back to you. I wanted more of you. Why did I stay again? While you were out entertaining other women and fucking them. Here I was trying to fix me for you instead of fixing me for me. In my mind, I was thinking you were being faithful to me, because you came home and told me that you loved me and only me, only to find out you were telling them the same. So, why am I here? I thought we had each other's back. I thought we were black love. Sorry, that was a fantasy, I was getting carried away in my thought. I thought we gave each other the world the best way we knew how. I thought we were loyal to each other. We gave each other wisdom and knowledge. So, was it all fake? I opened my world to you, I trusted you with my womb. I made sure life treated you well. So, why was I not good enough for you? So, you repay me by leaving me. Leaving me in the dark? How could you say you love me, but love someone else? How could you give them what we shared?

I thought my heart was for you. My heart never skipped a beat for you. I am trying to get myself together, but I am so hurt by the way things shifted between us. A precious part of me had left me spiritually to connect soulfully with yours. Now, what? I am left in a dark room, lonely, confused, and wondering why and how. Yes, I have said things to hurt you because I was tired of being hurt too. Now, we are both hurt and, in our feelings, and making decisions that will soon change our lives forever. I hope you are happy and that you find happiness. I hope she is all that you want, need, and dream of. I hope this new life brings you peace and joy. So do not worry about me and do not ever look back, because that chapter has closed. Now, that you have what you want, do not come looking for me telling me that you love me and that you have made a mistake. When things start looking good for me, do not say you wish you would have stayed to be a part of it.

When my grass starts getting greener, do not come by my side explaining why you could not water it and how hard it was to maintain it. My heart will land on someone else's hand, who will love me unconditionally. Love was beautiful when I was not being taken advantage of. It was beautiful when we were on the same page. You lead me on and created false feelings in me. You had me thinking our love was real. You played my faith with your deceitful self, moving me around as if I were the pieces in the chess game. It is okay. I will pick myself up again. I will be that and more, cut like a diamond and juicer like an olive. I will be more than enough for the one who can handle me, hold me, and love me right.

Is love a crime? Nowadays, love comes with a price. Love is blind. Love will have you looking foolish, doing foolish things, things you would never do. They put you through so much and find ways to manipulate you to stay. Love is so desperate. Why is love so blind? Love is so overrated. It will have you questioning love itself. The word hate is so strong, but I hate you for planting in me a cold heart. How more damaging can you be? Why is love so painful? How can love put you in rage? How can love be so violent? How can love be so detrimental to the mind, body, and soul? How can love causes you to forget who you truly are? How can love have you feeling lustful while lusting has you feeling as if you were in love? How can love be so powerful? Love should not have so many identities or personalities. Love comes from all angles. Love can be so premature when you think it's mature timing. Love can get you in trouble sometimes. Well, that's what I believe.

I became emotionally disconnected. I became heartless. I did not want anyone to love me because I would not be able to love them the way they loved me. I never experienced real love before, so whenever I built a close, genuine relationship with someone, I pushed them off because I was too scared of love. So, I became scared of letting them into my world. I was afraid of being loved by genuine people because I was too damaged to believe again. My personality was addictive because I had a vibrant spirit, a beautiful soul, and great a smile. To top it all off, my laughter, was a vibe by itself. At times, I may be flirty, but it is only because I am being playful in a funny way. My eyes are the best feature of me because they tell a story. And that is the most dangerous part of me because they can be flirty, misleading, and deceptive.

Can we talk about when I first met Dupris? My personality attracted him to me. My words channeled him into my world. After years of knowing him, I wanted to experience love for the first time

- with him. However, I was confused and battling between loving him and the life that I wanted to live. I was afflicted, but I knew he would be the one to remove my self-affliction and self-doubts. I knew his love would heal and help me to forget those open wounds. As we grew deeper, I started to reflect more on whether he will be able to add to the desires of my heart or give me the lifestyle I deserved. See, I love the finer things in life. I want a big house. A house of a millionaire with his and her bathrooms, a Jacuzzi, a sauna-type shower, a big backyard with a pool, for the future kids and the adults, a section for grill with a mini bar and flat-screen t.v., a big dressing room, a huge, walk-in closet, and stuff. I want to travel the world, waking up to a chef making three-course meals from time to time, and the banks knowing my name when they see me walk in, a big ring, not the traditional kind, just different. Living that millionaire status life. Yeah. That's what I deserve. Right?

Kind of like, living my celebrity lifestyle. I created this world inside me—that was my reality. It also boosted my self-esteem. I was Miss Independent, doing it big, according to me. In my reality, I was happy enjoying life. I wanted him to be a part of my world, so I led him on, and created this glamourous lifestyle so we could live in it together. I wanted what I wanted, and he took it away because he could not handle it. He felt I was living a lie, but I was not. It was me creating what I wanted. He felt that He had to dim my light because He could not find his own. He felt hurt by my actions, wait, how about yours. He made me feel worthless, unfulfilling, and endless.

So, let's talk about his ego. It is killing me and I am tired. I am tired of him taking my joy, lying to me, and then kissing me good night. He is burning me out, sucking the life out of me. Now, I have no voice to voice my pains and uncertainties. Like dude, can you even hear me? If he loves me, hear me. I cannot cry out to him anymore, my voice is dim, and my tears dried out. It is like talking to a brick wall. I have no voice to express to him how I feel. He killed every part of me, so there is nothing left in me; there are no remains. My heart is heavy, and I am choked up in pain. My heart left my chest chasing dreams of us healing while the pain was thrown back and forth without one to blame. I am living in confusion, not knowing where we would be, whether we were meant to be. I am losing myself, going crazy, thinking about suicide because I want out, or maybe if I killed myself things will get better. So, he regrets me? Well, dead me and *leave me alone!!*

How can God say you are the one for me when our relationship is spiraling and gone? So, when I get a prophecy, I question it. I start questioning God—is this the man for me or was I sleeping with the enemy? Am I really the woman for you? Because this relationship does not look like what God has promised. How can I stand on His Word when all of this is happening to me? How can he be the one for me when he does not see me the way he used to, he belittles me, and makes me feel worthless? How can we build a foundation together when the roots of our problems are getting dug deeper and deeper? You do not even respect me. You call me all kinds of names and create all kinds of memes in your head just to justify what you feel. How can it be?

When love becomes questionable, is it still love? I am still hurt knowing the problem that we are facing, we are dancing around it, and now it is becoming our drama- our reality. Questioning myself, "What did I sign up for?" Can we continue to pursue each other knowing the damage we have caused each other? Can we build on trust? Can we even look at each other the same, knowing the heavy loads we have put on each other? Do we take time apart? Do I even trust the process? Loving someone is loving them with all their flaws, taking all their wrongs, and making them right. Do you really love me? I love you more than words can express. I wish things can be better between us. It is killing me so deep inside that it hurts like a knife stabbing me inside and out. I apologize for what I have put you through. I did not love myself enough to have loved you. I took on the baggage of my past and brought it to you thinking I had my past under control when I moved forward by burying my issues alive. I tried to avoid facing it, but your past has a way of creeping itself in when not dealt with. I wish I could have put you first the way you put me first. I wish I were able to handle you with care the way you handle me with care. I should have been the shoulder you cried on instead of hers. I wish you would have understood me.

Now, my pride and feelings are in the way due to past hurt. If I knew how to love you, Dupris, I would have loved you instead of allowing my words to have pushed you away. Your words of anger pushed me towards wanting to love someone who I believe is not the one for me. I am still stuck on the fact that you cannot forgive me for the past pains I have caused you. You cannot trust me enough to see that I can and do love you. My ways were not sufficient to prove my love for you. The way you have treated me I could have treated you the same or better if you were just patient with me. Instead, you kept putting me in a rage and making me the angry black woman that I did not want to be. I was getting out of character, acting in ways that are uncalled for.

Unfortunately, we are two compassionate people giving mixed signals and in toxic positions. This is an unhealthy situation. We need to separate because we do not know how to love each other. My love has expired. Now, I have a damaged heart. I see why there is confusion in our relationship because you kept records of my past and questioned my love for you – putting expectations in our relationship hoping for me to fulfill the needs, the other women desperately did. The overall circumstances do not look like you're the man for me. I am tired. Tired of stalking your social media page trying to find out the truth. I am tired of checking your phone to see if you are still lying to me, tired of taking you back knowing that you will keep cheating on me, and tired of having anxiety attacks knowing my feelings are involved.

In my mind, all I want to do is hurt you more and move forward. A part of me is numb to all this pain. At times, I find myself wanting to be with someone else who deserves me and loves me. When you say you love me, I want to believe you love me. I struggle with the fact that I cannot trust you because you kept lying to me. So, let us end all our problems and MOVE ON!!! I promise to use what I have learned for the next man.

If God ordained you for me, then I will love you beyond measure. I will cherish you like I always imagined. Show off my love for you and do the things couples do. Be that Proverb 31 woman too you as he creates you to be an Ephesian 5 vs 25-33 husband. I will love you more and take away all the pain you had endured, during the years, and introduce you to something new. And brag about how great of a man you are to me, to show you how much of a KING you are. I will love you to pieces. It hurts to watch you go but I must let you leave.

If this process is going to make me a better person, I'll accept the journey and take accountabilities for all my actions and wrongdoings. Just know a part of me loves you deeply. I remember you'd quote the bible to me, saying, "Love is patient and is kind. Love doesn't envy. Love doesn't brag, is not proud, [5] doesn't behave itself inappropriately, doesn't seek its own way, is not provoked, takes no account of evil; [6] doesn't rejoice in unrighteousness, but rejoices with the truth; [7] bears all things, believes all things, hopes all things, and endures all things. [8] Love never fails. But where there are prophecies, they will be done away with. Where there are various languages, they will cease. Where there is knowledge, it will be done away with." (1 Corinthians 13 4-8 WEB). I am broken trying to find myself. You want me to love you again. Well, I can't because I am broken and in need of healing. I need space to heal.

DETOXIFIED MY SOUL Prayer

Dear God,

My soul needs cleansing – needs to be detoxified from the past. I need your spirit to exfoliate and remove all dead cells that have been clogging my heart, my mind, and spirit. I ask that you detoxified me; my soul. My heart hurt because I am in love with a man who hurt me deeply. I am having a hard time trying to let him go. I love him so much, but I know for sure he is too toxic for me. My heart is tied to him soulfully that I cannot let him go. I am trying so hard. It's not about the sex. I am stuck in the past, from when I first met him, the love he gave, his smile – his heart. It hurt more to see how he transformed into someone else. God, I know there's a lesson in this and you probably have someone better - waiting for me, ready to love me and show me the best side of life.

For him to release himself to me, I must heal and be ready for love- to love and be loved. At times, it is hard to accept he is not the one for me because I want him to be the one. As you remind me of how he does not appreciate me, cheat on me, verbally abuses me, fights in the past, talks bad about me to the women he deals with, and repeatedly comes back and walks out on me with no reason. HELL YEAH, I deserve better. I'll never forget that 3:00 am phone call from him, confessing that he is in love with me and his two side chicks. At that moment, it did not register with me, so I did not respond. Once I hung up, that's when the words hit my spirit and kept replaying in my head. My spirit started grieving. My heart became heavy. I started to get angry and think about millions of ways to f**** them up, especially that disrespectful chick. I was hurt, extremely hurt that I became bruised all over again. I questioned why I love this man. All he does is hurt me, and continuously hurt me.

Why do I yearn for a man that does not have respect for me? I invested so much in him, that it was that easy for him to walk without reasoning. Do I want him back? Yes, to the way it was when we first met. God forgive my heart and allow peace to be my portion while I wait on you, knowing that you will take care of me. You have something better in store for me. Renew my strength and repair my heart. This is so challenging, but I will overcome feeling that because I deserve better, and I will and shall have better. While I am waiting, I will continue to put you first. Just know I do not want to walk this journey alone anymore.

How do you love yourself? At times, we want to fill the voids caused by our past experiences. The real solution is being at peace with our past. We jump into relationships thinking this one will make up for the last one. When will we take accountability for our actions? When will we realize that every cause has an effect? The end of a relationship is the time to do some self-reflection before making someone else a victim. You tend to leave a trail, but never leave a positive imprint for someone to learn from. My question to you is what work have you done to heal what is within? Have you looked yourself in the mirror and asked why you are dealing with feelings of rejection or pain?

Childhood plays a huge role in creating those feelings. How were your parents' relationships? What was childhood like? The answer probably is not great. What moment stood out for you? How was elementary school? How was middle school or high school? What were your relationships with friends, a significant other, cousins, siblings, teachers, and others? Deliberately take the time to self-reflect on a situation that changed your life drastically.

Learn to acknowledge and use that pain and hurt towards something positive.

No one can love you the way you do. It's time to be responsible and stop creating victims. It's time to own up and apologize for your wrongdoings. It's time to be vulnerable and brave enough to make a change and live right because the energy you planted will follow you. It may not be the same kind of energy, but it will. We are beings made up of energy. What you send out into the universe will bounce back at you. The right love will find you if you don't ignore it. Sometimes it comes when you least expected it. If you find someone who loves you and meets you at your equilibrium, then the energy is right. If it doesn't vibrate, the energy is off. Things will always come to light. Things don't stay in the dark for too long. Watch the people you let into your heart because people make decisions that affect you.

Another tip. Some men are struggling with their past. However, do you love him with all your heart although he has a weakness? Depending on where you stand in the relationship and what you are willing to tolerate, you can decide what you want. It's either meet him where he is and help him to overcome his flaws and struggles or leave him alone and deal with someone who is mentally, physically, and emotionally strong enough to overcome his struggles. At the end of the day, a healthy healing process is the give each other space if both are at that capacity where we can't help each other heal. Instead of doing more damage to each other's mind, body, and soul.

Thank You Note to Him

Thank you for leaving me. Thank you for rejecting me. Thank you for walking away from my life. Reassuring me that I needed to know my worth. Thank you for not seeing the value in me. Thank you because I was able to see the bigger picture clearer now. I can see what I am, and the value that I hold. Thank you for making me see the qualities I should uphold. Thank you for allowing me to see myself for who I am. Thank you for helping me to be empowered and walk into my purpose and the power of the woman I am. Thank you for the pain because it birthed new gifts within. Thank you that I am now going to see the greatness in me and see beyond my limits. Thank you for helping me get in tune with my womanhood and fall in love with God's creation within me. Thank you. Thank you for pushing me closer to God.

Thank you for releasing me so the next man can enjoy everything that I am and will be. Thank you for releasing yourself so I can be in the hands of God to be placed in the right hands of who God ordained for my life. I will always pray for God to heal your heart, your mind, and your spirit and realize what you had is now gone. What you had would have taken you to the next level, the billionaire status would have been released within you, the greatness I saw within, no other will see it. Because they see the "right-now" but not the future. Thank you. Thank you. Thank you. With a loving heart, I release you to the hands of the love of you.

Thank you for allowing me to see myself for what it is. Thank you for allowing me to know that it is okay to remove the Miss. Independent garment and walk in my rightful place. Thank you for allowing me to see that a man with an open heart to love can secure you. Thank you for allowing me to see that being rejected is good, it is for my protection. Thank you for allowing me to draw closer to God, the best love....

PEP TALK FROM ME – PART I

Ever been so hurt that all you did was cry and had no words to explain how you felt inside as you watch the person keep hurting you and blaming you for their pain or afflictions because they can't see past their hurt? Ever been so hurt to the point that you started to talk down to yourself because you could have done better or had better if you weren't in the position or situation that you are in? When I look back at my life, I realized where I went wrong. I allowed certain people access to my life when I shouldn't have. I gave them too much of me. When you give someone too much of you, they take it and break you, to bring you down so you can't see the real potential in you. Instead of building you up, they break you down into pieces and manipulate you with their words to make you feel less because they don't feel they can amount to you or level up. What do they do to level up? They continue to bring you down and demolish those around you.

One thing I want to share with you is that even through your weakness you can build your strength, with prayer, counseling, and manifesting the life you foresee for yourself. I am not going to lie. It is not easy; it is a process. You must defeat the negative thoughts and give yourself pep talks to overcome and build your strength. If not, you will stay there stuck and *never, I mean never*, overcome that situation. I lacked in my prayer life although I knew I was supposed to pray. I manifest the negative because I allow what was in front of me to dictate my decisions and destination when I was supposed to manifest the opposite. I am going to be honest because I know my strength. I am the type that allows people to get me at my weakness because I know my strength will backfire on you. When I come out of that fire, that storm, I come out ten times stronger and better. You would think I had something to prove.

That's the favor of God within me. God will allow you to be in the fire and then allow you to come out like nothing ever happened. That's me. When the person thinks they have you mentally, physically, and emotionally, you come back stronger with all the things they said you couldn't do and do it better. That's the best reward. As I am writing this, I am writing with a smile because my comeback will be strong, and I see and feel it. My comeback will have people begging and apologizing that they overlooked me or did me wrong.

Your actions may not be perfect because we are humans who make mistakes and make poor decisions. People should never define who you are. God is a God of forgiveness, a God who takes your past and makes a better tomorrow from it. If you allow Him to do the work, I can tell you this much, God steps in to fix your problems. Sometimes if He doesn't act soon enough, we start to step in and then mess things up. God is not a man who needs our help to fix our situations because He does everything in His timing is not ours. He does a great job at handling our situations. I am learning to step back and let God take care of my enemies and of my painful situations because the greatest revenge is letting God take care of them. If you don't believe in God, well, let's say, let that negative energy go and let it take care of itself. At the end of the day, it will take care of itself.

Hopefully, by the end of the book, you will see whether you believe or not that there's only one God. Doesn't matter what you call Him. He is a Spirit, and He exists. We are spiritual beings, energy beings. What you release will be returned to you.

There were times I felt that I have failed myself and failed those around me that looked up to me. But one thing for sure is that those who love you will always love you and be there for you even through your blind moments. People may leave you alone for the moment but remember they will always have your best interest at heart. They want the best for you so they will leave you to improve throughout your journey. Find a song or a hobby that will minister to your spirit, meaning find something that will uplift your spirit during your hard times. Listening to the right gospel music daily helps me to feed my spirit, purge out, cry out, and release all the pain and hurt. For you, it may be rap music, gospel music, dancing, modeling, drawing, speaking to your counselor, or writing, whatever it is - as long as, it is healthy for the spirit.

PEP TALK FROM ME (Continuation)

I wonder if I am strong enough to walk away from this heartache and not give all my attention and energy to this situation. I wonder if I tell myself, "You got this; stay strong and move on." And I did. I wonder if I open my mouth and spoke positively over my life, and my life transformed. I wonder if I spoke against the strongholds in my life (the negative voices in my head), my thoughts would be renewed. I just wonder! Will I get my willpower back, the strength and peace that I've been yearning for? - Cassandra Edouard

When I look at the man in the mirror, I see a conflict of images and thoughts. The hardest thing is to mute the voices in my head. I don't want to speak negatively into the universe and release negative energy or forces into my life. I don't want to curse my future because life and death are in the power of our tongue. I want to overcome these life obstacles, but first I need to calm my mind and spirit- to feed them the right food and energy to dream big and work on my next move.

I don't want to attract trashy men; no-good men; womanizing men; uneducated men; no-standard men; string-along men; toxic men; boyish men; insecure men; low-life men; ungodly men; unspiritual men (not talking about religion), can't keep or hold a family man, no purpose men in my life. How are these men supposed to reflect me? They make me look degraded as if I didn't come from a family of morals and values. I'm not listing these things to say that I attract these types of men. I'm just speaking on the type of men that are out there. This list is not about all men because there are men out there who are doing what they are supposed to, who know how to value themselves, their identity, their character, their integrity, and their morals. They know when they bond with a woman and become one with her. They pick up, based on her reflection when the woman speaks volumes and has character. I am not asking or looking for a perfect man, but there are some things a man should know and do to keep his reflection sharp and looking good.

There are men out there who want to change and have a good heart, but who needs a strong woman to help them reach their full potential. There are genuine men out there who didn't come from certain lifestyles and therefore need a strong woman who can make them look good and give them a sense of value or become more valuable. They start to feel good about themselves because they have someone to represent them and stand by their side and give them that image they've been searching for—the ideal couple everyone wants to be. It boosts the man's ego and self-esteem to know that he could stand and is standing next to a strong beautiful, phenomenal woman. A man like that starts to value his woman even more and love her and treat her like the queen she deserves to be. Why? Because he knows her worth. She will forever be his diamond and we're not just talking about pearls and gold.

I don't want to lose myself anymore in the process of dealing with him because it cuts too deep that I'm no longer the strong woman that I used to be—the strong woman who meant what she said, and was able to walk away, and move on and focus on herself to better self and to do productive things. I found myself in a hole, a very deep hole, crying all the time about how I lost myself in the process of trying to gain knowledge of who I am as a woman and desire to become a better version of myself. I wished upon a star that I could go back to where I was because I was good there. I was comfortable and, for me, it was acceptable. I ask myself, is God trying to mold me to be better and bring in the new? Or is God trying to tell me something? Or is He pushing me in a direction to stretch me even more, so in the long run, and for whatever God-given purpose He has for me, I won't tolerate bullshit from anybody? Or is He telling me to run and leave my situation alone and let him work on things—my heart, my body, mind, spirit, and soul? I'm overwhelmed and I'm stressed. At times, I forget who I am and what I stand for, presently, I'm giving myself this pep talk because it's much needed to release every pain that I've been feeling for three damn years. I love myself more than I can even imagine.

But there's more that I want out of life. What I desire the most is not being played or feeling stuck and not having anywhere to run or hide. I need someone strong in my life that can take on my weakness and turn it into a strength. Someone I can call or come to whenever I'm out of myself. Someone who can teach me the deeper meanings of myself. Someone who can look into my soul and say, "Damn, girl, your life is gold, and it's forever a diamond because your spirit lasts a lifetime." This may sound corny, but it's true. So, the next time I will look at myself in the mirror and say great things because I can overcome the feelings that I feel. No man or woman can validate you; you have to validate yourself. No man or woman can love you the way you love yourself. So, the next time you want to cry because of how you feel inside, look in the mirror and define who you are. Stay strong and say proudly and deeply how you feel about yourself. You don't want to be stuck in a situation that you feel you can't come out of, but you must decide on the direction you want to go.

I don't want to live in confusion anymore. I don't want to worry about him being unfaithful to me because of his insecurities. I don't want to be accountable for his past, just his present and his future. So, if he knows we can't last, leave and let someone who can speak life come to my lifeless self and bring life to me.

There's a saying that the opposite attracts. They attract for a reason. When a man meets a woman and is attracted to her, it's because her character speaks volumes. It's not to intimidate a man or make him feel less than. She's a reflection of you; she's making you look good by standing next to you and giving you volumes.

THE POWER IN SELF-INVESTMENT, WOMEN

"So many of us invest a fortune making ourselves look good to the world, yet inside we are falling apart. It's time to invest on the inside."

— Iyanla Vanzant

How many of us have listened, used, or taken our advice to better ourselves, the relationships we have with others, or our lives in general? We are so quick to play the role of victim and attack being authentic, but behind closed doors, we are as fake as a disposable plate. We live a lie because we can't face the real deal. We can't accept who we truly are because we lost our sense of self. We are not true to ourselves until we unmasked who we truly are. Women are valuable and a gift from God. Your world is so precious and beautifully created. You are wonderfully made in the image of the Creator, God. You are a true goddess and a true queen. You are an investment, a treasure, a creator, a power source, a scarce resource, a healer, a peace temple. YOU ARE LIFE, A STRONG VOICE, ENDEAVOR TO BE YOUR OWN VOICE. BE YOUR OWN KIND of VOICE. Nothing is more powerful than your voice. As women, we are very strong human beings who carry so much weight on our shoulders. We are intelligent, and have beautiful vibrant spirits; our souls are mystical, loving, and genuinely caring.

By nature, we can bounce back and become ten times stronger than when we were broken. We carry life and bring life into this world. We don't have or need to tolerate anything or anyone because we deserve all that our heart desires. Let's put ourselves first. Step into your authority and take authority over your life. Always evaluate your day and intentions; they will help you gain clarity and unmask the true feelings of the inner you. Listen to that deeper voice inside of you; it will guide you to the right path. Your intuition will never fail you. Just don't operate in your feelings; it will cause you to make temporary decisions. At times, we give ourselves these pep talks and end up believing what we think. Don't lie to yourself. Don't make assumptions. Our heart knows what is best. Trust in yourself in making good decisions to remove toxic situations.

In the words of Iyanla Vanzant, "Know your worth and do not accept the unacceptable because people will hold you to your limitation, they will hold to what they believe about you. Do not accommodate or tolerate what does not honor you." This goes for any kind or type of relationship—whether it's a friendship, an intimate relationship, a relationship in the job, a personal relationship, or a business relationship; it speaks to all relationships. According to G.L Lambert, "Become an empowered woman to get a powerful result." Let go of those toxic relationships. Don't allow yourself to keep being hurt. Why do you keep living in hurt and keep creating that same cycle that you can't seem to break? When it is time to be happy, we can't accept it because we are looking to be hurt again. When we see a red flag, either we pack our bags and go or fix it, depending on the circumstances. You will know what you should and shouldn't do or allow. Yes, you are allowed to say I'm done. Do what is best for you, what works for you, not what someone else says will work for you. It's about you. There's nothing wrong with advice, but no matter how many people give their opinion or advice, it's still about you and what will work for you. At the end of the day, they are not living your life for you.

As women, we allowed the glass ceiling of a man to shame us because the man doesn't understand where we come from and how we were raised and what we've been through to build our character. He doesn't understand that we won't tolerate a lot of the things that they do to us. Then the man starts playing the manipulating game and he starts to want us to sympathize by playing the victim card or blaming us for things he witnessed or has been through. I want to say you're brave and you are a strong woman even when you think you're not. In the Bible, it says even at your weakest, you are strong (2 Corinthian 12:9). The fact that you're still here and you're able to go through and be a phenomenal strong woman for someone else, allowed you to gain ten times the strength that you never thought you would gain. You are not in this battle alone because there are other women out here going through exactly what you're going through, some worse. You just gave them confirmation, strength, access, and the ability to move forward and never look back. And if they do, they can refer to what you went through just to have a piece of something to hold onto, knowing there is hope on the other end by taking a leap of faith and speaking life into their life.

When you think your life is lifeless, you just add more life into your life. So, what are you going to do differently? Are you just going to mourn and be sorrowful for the rest of your life or are you going to pick up and start creating steps to a better life? Find out what matters to you the most. Is it your body? Is it your parents? Is it the way you dress? Is it your hair? Is it your character? Is it your finances? Is it the people that you want to attract? Is it your heart? Is it your weight? Create a goal and master it.

Once you master that goal, you start feeling good about yourself, then you will have the courage and willpower to overcome any life challenges. I'm pretty sure once you look good and you became that ideal woman you created for yourself, everything else will fall into place. It takes time and discipline. You will fall short, but just give yourself credit for the small steps you have taken to better yourself and life. Don't let anyone make you feel otherwise. You don't need to be in a relationship to be happy or feel great about yourself or reinvest in yourself. You can be married and still feel way less worthy and have low- self-esteem. And don't be moved by what society say. media plays picket fences because it doesn't even stand up for itself.

Behind the scenes, people promote false and negative news to you just so the news can be a trend and they can get paid more and get higher viewers or ratings. Society is also lost and not awake. That's why society has people thinking about it and following what's trending.

These people don't even know what's trending within themselves, so they want to follow the crowd and jump on the bandwagon until they drown. If they knew what to follow and who to follow, their comments and the statements that they make wouldn't promote negativity. If anything, they would be uplifting and bring everyone together to make the world a better place. So, find a crowd that speaks to you because everyone has a character or trait that speaks to a specific crowd. For example, Cardi B speaks to a specific crowd, Beyonce speaks to a specific crowd, Lady Gaga speaks to a specific crowd, Solange speaks to a specific crowd, Janelle Monae speaks to a specific crowd, Jhene Aiko speaks to a specific crowd, Mariah Carey speaks to a specific crowd, Erykah Badu speaks to a specific crowd and Ariana Grande speaks to a specific crowd. Each of these women speaks to a different crowd, but does it take away from who they are and what they produce. Nor does it take away from them as icons.

The point is that your personality doesn't sit well with everybody, and you can't mix and mingle, and try to make everyone proud because you can never, please everyone; you can only please yourself, and God. You will attract those that are like-minded as you. Be yourself. Find your crowd and stick to it. Your authenticity will make room for you and attract individuals who understand and are motivated and encouraged by your language or your character, and the ways you speak to people. They will respect you for being you. And even if they don't agree with you. There are a billion people in this world that you will speak volumes to, and you will change their lives because you motivate them and help them change their lives. They will look up to you and will do things that you do.

This is the reason why God is molding your character, so naysayers can't affect you and you can ignore them. Yes, it's hard to ignore the naysayers because you're on a mission or an assignment. But why are you trying to prove anything to them when they don't have anything to prove themselves? We all have skeletons in our closets, and some people are not ashamed to reveal themselves because, in their minds, they are too naive to see the wrong. At the end of the day, they don't pay your bills, they don't put food on your table, they don't manage or handle events in your life and they didn't bring you into this world. So, there is no way they can take you out. You don't wake up with them, you don't sleep with them. You don't smile with them; you don't chat with them. They're not part of your circle. Even if they were, their opinions don't matter because, nine times out of ten, they are irrelevant. They can say whatever they want or feel, because, at the end of the day, their negativity is a fertilizer, that is pushing you to your destiny, to your purpose, and to where you need to be.

No disrespect to men, but we don't *need* a man to have the life we desire, want, or need. We need to first build ourselves and complete ourselves in order to have a man in our life. Build your home *before* a man comes in. He will respect you more and would love to build a foundation together. There's a difference between thinking a man is a want and a need. It's simple—one woman thinks a man is an answer to all her problems, and the other woman solves her problems.

Let's play a game. I'm going to provide you with some synonyms of the words "want and need"- then add "a man" to it. Then you can choose whether you want or need a man. Ready? WANT: desire a man, wish for a man, hope for a man, have a fancy for a man, have an inclination for a man, care for a man, like a man, set one's heart on a man, long for a man, yearn for a man, pine for a man, sigh for a man, crave a man, hanker after a man, hunger for a man, thirst for a man, lust after a man, cry out for a man, be desperate for a man, itch for a man, covet a man, be bent on a man, have a yen for a man, and be dying for a man. For most of us women, we have already been there or done that for the man that we love or they either made us crazy, confused, or been bent over backward, doing such crazy things.

Now let us do the word NEED: require a man, need a man, stand in need of a man, have need of a man, want a man, crying out for a man, be desperate for a man, demand a man, call for a man, require a man, entail a man, involve a man, have occasion for/to a man; lack a man, be without a man, be short of a man, miss a man, be under an obligation to a man, be obliged to a man, be compelled to a man, and be under a compulsion to a man. Well, in this situation it seemed we've been in these situations as well. So overall, which do you prefer? Was it better to want or need a man?

After hearing that, I bet some of you are probably thinking, "Oh, I need a man! I don't want a man, honey!" Did you get it? Was that a little fun or a fun game to play? Next time, try doing this with your friends, co-worker, or a group and see what everyone else's position is. Honestly, we want a man in our lives; he is not a need. Yes, it is not good for a woman or a man to be alone. The point of this is you don't need a man in your life to feel complete. You can complete that on your own. Have a man in your life to add to what you bring to the table. You should see him as an asset, not a liability. He should not want or be treated like a CEO with janitorial background, janitorial mentality, janitorial requirements, or janitorial title. Please forgive me, nothing wrong with being a janitor. The point is he should not be treated like a husband if he did not put a ring on it. He should not be treated like a King; if he does not know how to treat you like a Queen.

Take the time to define how important a man is to your life. How does he define you? Or represent you? At the end of the day, you are his favor – meaning you are his "proverbs 31 woman." He should find you, not you finding him. For example, for me, I want him to be my protector, I want to feel secure mentally, physically, financially, and emotionally, and I want him to be my sanctuary and my third eye for when I can't see clearly. These are important to me because I want to feel a sense of security. Some people will say you can give yourself that. Yes, you can, to a certain degree, but the beauty comes when a man can give you that as well. It is like a Lion protecting his jungle and his family. The lion has power and strength. A lion maintains order, maintains balance, is in control, and stands in command. Like the lioness, she is also a protector, a provider, and a loving mother to her cubs. She is extremely independent and ambitiously driven but when it comes to her family, she empowers the lion and showers the cubs with extreme love and care.

When my King or man is a representation of what I am looking for? It raises a vibrant side as a woman and makes you feel like a woman—his woman—and secure in your position when he plays his part and makes you feel secure. On another note, I will say this—know your self-worth, know what you want and need within yourself first before you start saying what you want or need in a man or from a man. Become what you want and desire and you will attract it. You must establish yourself, reinvent yourself, and find your self-worth. Iyanla Vanzant said it best, "MASTER YOU and GROUND YOURSELF spiritually, every day" (Vanzant, Iyanla. July 23, 2017. https://youtu.be/jzLSsmZXTms).

In order, to be a better you, you must:

1. Practice feeding your spiritual self daily- making time to pray to have a spiritual connection and relationship with God, your creator.

2. Doing inner healing – soul searching (go through the process, do not hinder yourself, practice daily soul-cleansing).

3. Go on a Fast (fast from people, social media, phones anything that is a distraction, and negative energy).

4. Forgive yourself and others (give yourself time to do and not give them your energy).

5. Be patient with yourself (it's a process).

6. Be truthful- honest with yourself (address the issues, concerns, and feelings).

7. Change your thoughts.

8. Put yourself first.

9. Know your worth.

10. Know who you are (finding your identity and accepting it).

11. Be clear about your boundaries.

12. Don't accept the unacceptable.

13. Unpack that baggage. Ask for what you want and don't settle for something lesser. Don't settle for things that will dim your light.

14. Trust God and yourself.

15. Use feedback to improve (positive and purposeful feedback).

As we reflect on ourselves and focus more on our inner healing. We must do some deep cleansing; this is the time to really release the old feelings and energy as well as folks. As women, we should reflect on ourselves we should not allow a man or anyone else to disrespect or devalue our character, belittle our intelligence, and reinvent our womanhood. Remember, your values don't lie in someone else's hands. We need to learn to stand firm and set goals for ourselves and follow through. We are like a cellphone and men, or friends are the features—the additional features. Don't let any man take away from your self-worth. Not all men are jerks or fools, but the ones that are, have a HIStory of brokenness, which may have started from childhood. Examine their past relationships, their relationship with both parents, especially with their mother, siblings, and their parents' relationship. Look at their circle of friends. Question and observe these things. What you see, is what *you* will get. They will show you their true colors. Watch. You will see. At times, they may follow the footsteps of their parents, and, or be the opposite of their parents.

This is not to bash men because there are women who do the same. This is to remind women of who they are and where they came from. It's alright to be different and unique and love the skin you are in. It's alright to be broken and put back together again. A vase can break multiple times but once repaired the correct way, that glass becomes brand new and has a different effect and look. Everything is recycled and so are we. One man's trash is another man's treasure. Just don't allow yourselves to be with the wrong kind of man or continue to accept or attract the same kind of man that hurt you; do not know your self-worth- to the point you lose who you are and who you worked hard to be.

Keep your integrity as a woman and stand up for YOU and in what you believe - even when you are emotionally weak, stuck, and hurt. Prepare yourself to be in the process of being in repair. Remember this, it takes honesty, bravery, and courage with oneself to get back up again and put yourself back together again. G.L. Lambert said it best, "Be who you truly are and not based on your egotistical view of yourself." Sometimes, if a person cannot meet you where you are or you cannot meet them where they are, maybe you just need to leave them. You must stand on your Yes and stand on your No. If that man is or for you, he will come back. If he does not. He was not for you. Let him be someone else's headache and stress and if he is not their stress then that's fine. You guys were not a perfect match. remember he was not meant for you. You cannot force an unfit puzzle to fit.

Another thing—if a man cheats, he cheats on himself and not on you. Check his record, how did you meet him? Do you see a patterning in his behavior? If so, expect it to be a continuation of the same thing unless he changed. So, why continue to repeat the same cycle of hurt and pain? When a man is doing this, it is because he is insecure, angry, lacking love or self-love, in need of validation, low commitment, rejected or neglected, dealing with his past, has a weakness, can't control himself, or maybe not sexually satisfied, selfish - and I am pretty sure there are other reasons as well. Though people say when a man cheats it is due to emotional voidness. But that does not mean you tolerate his behavior. A person chooses to cheat and makes excuses as to why they cheat. Save yourself from the headache, of being exposed to his selfish act and leave.

A book I would like to recommend to you ladies, *Men Don't Love Women Like You*, by G.L. Lambert. This book will help you go from placeholder to game changer. Don't allow your hurt or misunderstanding to hurt someone else. Ladies, always acknowledge and accept your feelings about where you are. It takes time, but I promise you, towards the end, you will feel restored, renew, confident, wise, empowered, encouraged, and brave. You'll have a new set of attitudes with qualities attached to them. YOU ARE QUALITY! YOU ARE AN INVESTMENT! As you start regaining your strength, you will feel like a priority and not an option. You will carry yourself with modesty and walk in your authority. It will feel so good and so refreshing when you can take authority over your own life especially if you're coming from a broken relationship or finding yourself again. It takes courage to get up and leave and say it's over. It takes strength to walk out that door and not look back. Sometimes, it's okay to ask for space or time apart for a better relationship.

At times, space is needed for both parties to work on their well-being. It's a part of finding your happiness, making peace with yourself, loving yourself, doing what *you* love, and not allowing people or society or social media to define your self-happiness. You know YOU! BE YOU! Sometimes, taking time apart means never coming back. It's okay because people outgrow each other, or the relationship did not work. Sometimes, we are so lost in each other that we forget what makes us happy, and we forget what it's like to smile, be healthy, or have a great time. We are too focused on making our spouse happy or comprising too much that we lose ourselves in the process. A balance is needed to make a relationship work. I was watching the Red Table Talk; a talk show, starring actress, Jada Pinkett Smith- the wife of actor Will Smith. Will Smith and Jada Pinkett said something that stood out to me, "Deconstructing to reconstruct is the best way to go." Sometimes, it takes letting go and doing some soul searching to come into a relationship, not expecting, but understanding, this is you and this is me, and being able to respect what makes that individual happy.

Will Smith said something so profound during the Red Table Talk when discussing their challenges in their relationship, which I believe would be helpful. He stated, "One day, I'll do what makes you happy and next time I'll do what makes me happy, even when it's repetitive or boring." That's what makes a relationship authentic, as well as healthy- doing what works and what is best for you and your partner or spouse. When you have too many mouths speaking, they start to fertilize negative seeds that cause your relationship plant to lack potential growth.

Lastly, we need to know when enough is enough. Be able to love yourself enough to say that is it. Why continue to live in hurt when there is a way out and I'm not talking about suicide? I'm pretty sure someone is waiting to take his/her place. A way out doesn't always mean, throwing it all away. It can mean taking a break to come back with giving that unconditional love or it may mean not coming back at all. I understand that in some relationship, he took you in and you left your home or your parents' home to be with him or you love him and don't want to lose him, or you have nowhere to go. Maybe you can't return home because you will be shameful. You are willing to stay and stick with it. In most cases, love doesn't keep us safe. It will either kills us or make us stronger. Why wait until the last minute to find your soul wandering around when you could have avoided it? We are too afraid to lose our comfort zone because we think we won't or can't find something better. There's always better on the other side. It's either you leave to better yourself or you leave to find better. We try to stay in a relationship that doesn't fit. It's like putting an unfit puzzle together. If it does fit, it takes time to find the perfect fit. If it's meant to be, it will be. Love will always find its way back to you.

To create or have a strong foundation, it must be reconstructed, broken down, and rooted to be built back up strong again. The point of it all is knowing your worth and not letting anyone or any man strip that away from you. Don't give anyone too much power over you that you lose your integrity. Get up and get out. You will never know the outcome or the support you have until you step out and save yourself and your family. Sometimes, what may have been ugly can turn out to be the best thing. The universe or God has a way of aligning the right people in your life to help you get over situations or circumstances in a time of need. It's up to you to be willing to follow through, follow your intentions, or the deeper voice saying do it. Some of us are not as lucky as others. It is hard being in a situation and having no one to call or attend to you because they are miles away, so you feel stuck.

Therefore, in the time of sorrow, map out and plan each day until you have something that will help you. Google resources or local organizations, centers or non-profits organizations, or charities that can help you. If that's not the route you want to take in the storm, start saving money, look for another place to live, or plan a vacation; just *map it out*. The initial outcome may be ugly, but the long-term results shall be better. You just must believe in yourself when making a change. Sometimes the best teacher, while you are going through something, is yourself. Speak life into yourself and roar.

Change your environment, it will change your circumstances. If you find yourself going circles in a new relationship, that is the same pattern of conduct, then the problem is within you. It's time to reconstruct yourself. Sit down and revisit your mistakes. Find out why you are going in circles. There's something you did that you didn't fix or change. *Love thyself. Keep your head above water. Never let a man see you drown* unless he is willing to save you and bring you above water. Keep in mind that a strong woman needs a strong man so when she becomes weak, he can make her strong again.

Bonus: what God ordains for your life, no matter what you are facing, what is for you is for you. Just pray and meditate and keep the faith. It's not easy but trust the process because it shall turnaround. When God promises you something or someone, know that it shall happen in due time.

Quick Gem:

Do not comprise your happiness for someone else's happiness. Do not settle because you think or believe that is all you can have or deserve. I know it gets hard and lonely. Trust me. God will never fail you. He will give you what is best for you verse what you think is best. He will give you the desires of your heart based on needs and not wants. Do not settle for whatever reason. If you did. Take it back. Take back what you settled for and pray. Take back your happiness, your joy, and your life. What God has for you or ordained for your life. NO ONE can come against it, steal it, take it away, rob you for it, or manipulate you. And ask God for a double with an upgrade and interest. You deserve real love.

I want you to imagine yourself being with the man who hurt you and or caused you pain. Imagine settling just to keep him around for temporary love, temporary healing, temporary sexual needs- knowing that he won't change or love you the same. Imagine lying next to him and he is texting another woman, and you barely get a text or a conversation. Imagine him saying, I will call you back and he does not. Just to speak to another woman for hours. Imagine him saying, I love you just to see or find pictures of him loving another woman. Imagine him saying I got something for you just to make you smile and find out what he had for you was for someone else he loved and trusted. Just imagine all that pain and hurt, you are trying to get over. You recreated over and over again thinking, hoping, and praying for a better result. The only result is a broken heart, trauma, open wombs, cuts, and bruises. You are keeping them around for what? Just to fulfill a temporary void or prove your love for them. Why temporary- why have it for a limited time? When you can have someone or something **forever – unlimited**. Ask yourself this question, then what? After that temporary void is fulfilled, what is next? Now what? You kept them around just to return to the trauma, the pain, the hurt, the lies, the drama, the cheating, the disloyalty, their disfunction, their insecurities, lack of support, their displeasure for you, that makes you feel unworthy, mishandled, misused, abused verbally, physically, and emotionally, raped, robbed, rejected, betrayed, talked about, taken advantage of, cursed out, and all of the extra unnecessary baggage. To use all of your energy arguing, screaming, breaking and vandalism, crying, the confusion, searching the phone, unkept promises, calling friends, the lying, getting dressed to prove a point, or him calling his friends to clown you. How he got you or can take advantage of you.

Why waste energy when you can save that. Now you'd have created more wombs on top of open wombs, and you wonder why you cannot be healed. Because you have decided to pile up hurt on top of hurt, trauma on top of trauma because you think you cannot have better or just don't want to start over. Or maybe that is how you see yourself as? When you look in the mirror that is all you see, know, and have become, so you become accustomed to it, accept it, and live in it. Listen to this, that does not define you, you do not deserve that. Why would you want to comprise your happiness, love, your identity, and who you are to keep someone around that won't reciprocate the same. Who does not see you as their reflection or complementary to their life? Do not love you the same way or feel the same about you. They would and will show other people the same love you've been crying, pleading, begging, and asking for. Why would you want a person, who disrespects you over family and/or friends, someone who just keeps putting you through constant shame? All those red flags and yet you're still in it, you want to go back praying and hoping for a better result. You wonder why you cannot heal properly but you are opening too many doors, and creating easy access for continuous heartbreak, to be a target and prey to your predator. You accept all these ill-treatments only to suppress the feeling of being alone. God is always speaking to us, but we tend to ignore His voice, the signs, and our spirit man. When God is in the process of giving you something better, he prepares you for it. He creates in you a new heart, a new woman, a new man within you so he can release you to where or to whom he is sending you.

The work must be done within you, inside of you. It is an inside job, but you must first MENTALLY, be ready, prepared, and WILLING to go through the transformation – meaning the brokenness, being gracefully broken to be that wife or husband for the future spouse; to be that business partner, that preacher, teacher, director, apostle, bishop, whatever position he has for you. It is a process – for wisdom, knowledge, and revelation to be downloaded and given to you. If you are scared to let go or afraid to move forward. That means you are saying to yourself that you don't deserve greater and better things in life. You are telling yourself I do not have what it takes to go to the next level and chapter of my life. I am not ready to be the woman or man God is creating me to be or evolved to be. This is when you look at yourself in the mirror and tell yourself you are better than this. You can have better and start creating within yourself first, what it is that you are looking for.

God is funny, he loves us so much he will strip us away from people, places, and things just to get our attention to say YOU DESERVE BETTER. STOP SETTLING FOR LESS. I HAVE BETTER FOR YOU. I NEED YOU. I AM YOUR FIRST LOVE. Seek me first, the kingdom of God and all things (everything, the desires of your heart) will be added onto you. You must first realize it for yourself. Believe it and trust God. While he is making us whole again, he is molding us into the person he wants us to be so we can have peace, joy, love, happiness, and the fullness of life. Then we can share it with the man or woman he has ordained for our lives. Trust me, God knows how to make us smile at the right moment and place. His timing is not our timing so wait on Him and be still. While waiting, work on yourself, that body, your health, your mind, and your beauty. Do things you have never done before, get a new job with a great salary, go on trips, work on your business or books, get that house, build your credit, get to work, and stick to it. Bounce back and then watch it work. Level up, upgrade, it is in your bounce back, you will see your strongest comeback.

Lastly, I shared this on Facebook. God said this to me as I was writing it. Remember this, when God gives us a revelation to share, at times, he is speaking to us in future or present tense/ situation. Always go back to messages or words, you wrote because it can help you get through. Here is the word on March 16, 2022, at 8:10 am EST: "Most of us go back to the past of what was and try to resuscitate what was dead. God is saying in this season. What he allows to die, doesn't need to come back to life. Stop trying to revive what was when I'm trying to give you something new. I allowed it to happen the way it did for a reason. There is something I'm trying to give you. It's better than what you think you had. You'll be very happy once you see what is in my hands concerning you."- Cassandra Edouard

Let the past be the past. Let go and TRUST GOD. It is a mental thing, some of us say it but do we believe it, can we do it!!! And be for real.

PEP TALK to THEM

When the past come towards you, face it, and take responsibility for your actions. One thing though—don't let it define you. You probably made poor decisions in your life that you can't get away from because something or someone keeps reminding you of it. Have you ever felt or have been convicted for something you've done in your past, and had to face the judge to let him know the truth with all your evidence and it still wasn't enough to support your claim? Because of a poor decision that you've made in your past, you are still being convicted for it. People happen to overlook the good that you have done or that you've changed for the better and are a better person. Instead, they are in the past that they miss the great blessings present before them. You have to do time, so you take accountability knowing that, in the end, God will make all things new. He will take the bad and create all new things, and good things out of the situation. You may have been convicted, but God said that all those times you were convicted, He counted and created something great for you, for the circumstance is to better you and not to harm you. Jeremiah 29:11 says, "For I know the thoughts that I think toward you," says Yahweh, "thoughts of peace, and not of evil, to give you hope and a future." (WEB). Have faith and know that you have been forgiven even when a person judges or doesn't forgive you. True repentance in the eyes of God comes with a reward.

The best thing I have done was seek counseling to help me heal from the past, to help me become a stronger woman able to face every adversity in my life. I choose a Christian counselor. Why? Because I needed someone who was in tune with God and who could hear from God concerning me. I needed someone who could give me great counseling that could pour into my spirit to uplift me. Yes, I went to church and I have a great support system, but for me, that wasn't enough. I need to hear one voice and that was the voice of God. I had too many people in my ears, too many voices speaking to me, and too many messages. I had to stop everyone and listen to one voice. Thus far, counseling has helped me overcome my greatest fear and helped me become the greatest version of myself.

Counseling has helped me to become a greater person. Now, I am walking in my purpose. My gifts are making room for me. I am happier, healthier, wiser, and at peace. I have everything I want and desire because I made peace with myself. I changed what was and made it what it shall be. I looked at the man in the mirror and made a change for the better. Now, I have my house, my family, and a wife to an amazing KING. I have a million-dollar business, a non-profit organization, am a best-selling author, and speak and teach young women all over the world.

(Understand now…it's only been one session, but I am already speaking this into existence because life and death are in the power of our tongues; see Proverbs 18:21). What you speak shall be manifested. I foresee myself doing bigger and greater things. I am writing this so when I looked back, I will have a huge smile knowing that this came true!

TRUST IN YOU AGAIN

Trusting yourself again is a process, trusting that you can confide, feel safe or secure, and protect yourself. First, we must master self-healing. In order, to trust you again, we must master trusting in ourselves by doing a deeper inner cleansing. What does it look like? Seeking God to mend (repair) your broken heart, and bind and heal every open womb. Accepting and acknowledging what happened to you, the emotions you felt during the time or moment, and not questioning why. It is the why that brings back the feeling, the anger, the sadness, the bitterness, the hurt, and the pain that we felt- because we feel we did not deserve it. Yes, you are right. No one, not even the perpetrator, the betrayer, the victimized one, deserves it as well. No one deserves to cause the pain, revisit the pain, recycle the pain, return the pain, and retraumatized the situation all over again. It caused you to be stuck in the place you do not deserve to be in and want to revisit with yourself or with anyone else. The problem is if we do not let go and heal. We will repeat the hurt and pain all over again. Keep this in mind, your trauma has trauma, when you are experiencing multiple traumas such as abuse, (physical, emotional, verbal, systematic), rape and molestation, witnessing death, being institutionalized, losing a loved one, betrayal, cheated on, lied on, being exposed, and the list goes on - that you have not dealt with for the first time.

It will cause you to rebirth, self-sabotage, and be victimized by the situation that kept you abound. It is like being a slave to and then enslaving others into your traumatic experiences. Not only that. It will result in you operating in negative behaviors (actions and words), view people as hidden agendas with judgments of wanting to guard and protect yourself- causing you not to trust, to shut down, escape, live in uncertainty, feel overwhelmed, and alone. Some people may be born into trauma (ex: being born with Aids, given up for adoption- physical separation due to death or violence or something you cannot control). Growing up with that trauma results in feeling hopeless, damaged, confused, and living in regret. You get stuck in your thoughts, thinking of ways to learn to cope with the experience that grows deep inside.

As we are learning to redeem ourselves from that inner pain and reestablish who we are. Redeeming is crying it out, writing it out, talking it out, praying it out, dancing it out, whatever you need to do to purify and cleanse the soul to release what you were feeling. It is imperative to trust what life is trying to teach and tell us- meaning communicating to us. Only to regain and rebuild the trust within us. We must relearn to learn and reconnect to connect with the inner self to heal, trust, care, and love again. These things are needed to elevate and evolve to be the individual you were created to be. Once we deal with it and continue to practice healing, we will see what you were facing and how it became a strong hold in your life. Whether we were broken, bruised, bleeding, abused, or shattered into pieces, we must seek healing to heal. You desire to be made whole and to be fulfilled. The beauty of this process is being able to accept that we are gracefully broken like in the song by Tasha Cobbs. We can heal and will become stronger individuals. The essence of this is God is willing to give us beauty for those ashes. How can He do that? If we continue to hurt ourselves by going back to the places and people that hurt us and caused us pain and the reasoning to not trust ourselves and others.

We trust people for us verse trusting us for people. Trust is a process, but it starts within. When we make up in our minds to heal, to be delivered from the past, ourselves, and our broken hearts, God will see us through. Secondly, if we pray for God to remove the pain and he did not, it is because he is birthing a gift inside of us and allowing us to go through to show us that he was with us the whole time and brought us through. If you are wondering where to start. The process starts within, addressing all the hidden issues, knowing that it is not going to do any good holding onto who, what, when, where, and how it hurt you, knowing that it was necessary. And lastly, not focusing on the wrong, right, or fairness, but focusing on taking accountability for what we are allowed. That's where the Trust process begins.

Trusting the process is knowing that when there is a calling in your life. You will be going through some things, because of the anointing of your life. When God is calling you whether to be a proverbs 31 woman, a businesswoman, a preacher, teacher, an apostle, a prophetess, a director, or a millionaire. Whatever position God has ordained for your life, it is going to cost you. Do you trust yourself enough to go through the storm or your brokenness? God wants to give us something better, such as to evolve to be the finer and better woman He created us to be. He wants to bring us out.

Self-Talk: I robbed myself of true love by not properly loving me, healing me. I wanted the relationship that everybody else had just to say I have a man. Not realizing a relationship came with work. The kind of work that one's need to be healed in order to handle pure love. I should have healed from past hurt before entering a relationship because all I did was attract hurt and pain. And true love does not hurt. Trusting in you again requires self-healing, real self-love, and exercising self-worth. What does that look like? Healing from what have hurt you that inner child needs love, study you, putting yourself first - not letting no one or anything come between me, myself, and I, creating healthy boundaries and space for yourself, be okay with saying no, set the mood or tone, and do not let anyone rob you of your true happiness. Focus on you mind, body, and soul, what makes you feel good inside and outside. Get up! Get dolled up, go out and enjoy a good time with you. Get to know and love you. Don't forget to look in the mirror and remind yourself how dope you are. Speak great affirmations and say I am more than enough. Do things that makes you happy, sing, dance, laugh, exercise, vacation, travel, do your hair and make-up, go to the movies, read, dress up, go to events, cook, paint, write, journal, attend plays, accomplish a task or a goal, meditate, pray, buy plants, take naps, drink wine, shop- just don't go broke and most importantly validate yourself.

Some may feel they do not know what they deserve because they have been broken. The answer is you do. Every time you scroll on social media, you see something appealing to the eye. You say to yourself this should have been me or could have been me or this is what I want. Or you live your life through other stories. It is a reminder that you deserve this too. God gives us the desires of our heart, but we must do the work and wait patiently. You can have it. If you desire it for you, not for selfish gain. Most importantly, heal that inner child, redefine she, and do it well. Regroup, Reset, Reboot, and bounce back. And promise to never look back. Remember to never settle for less than what you truly deserve. Close that chapter and Trust in you again.

NO PAIN NO GAIN

Betty Wright, an American soul and R&B singer, songwriter, and background vocalist – stated in her song No Pain No Game, "Anything worth havin' at all is worth workin' for and waiting' for. We all are entitled to make mistakes."

A man will love who he loves. A man will marry who he feels is the one for him. You can't change how he feels about you, no matter what you do or how honest you are about your situations. Some things are better to take to your grave. At the end of the day, you can't force a man to love you or give you what he is not ready to give you. At the end of the day, if he is for you, he will change his ways. If he doesn't, it's either one or two things: he is not ready to be with you or he is still searching for his soulmate. Don't fight for a relationship that is not meant to be. Let him go and let him be. If he keeps saying he wished he could be with an ex, due to whatever reason, consider that, that 1. He is confused. 2. He does not love you. 3. He is missing a piece of that woman you cannot fulfill. 4. He is dealing with insecurity and looking for many women to fulfill his needs. 5. You will never satisfy him. A man that loves a woman will give her an understanding of where the relationship lies. He won't keep hurting you and making you feel less than.

This is not all men because he who finds a wife; finds a good thing and doesn't have to keep searching. A man that keep searching didn't find what he is looking for. Or thinks that if he was with such-in-such, life would be much better. There's nothing you can say to change his mind. If you can truly change how he feels based on your actions, command your change. If you try all the above and nothing good happens, let it go. I know it is hard to let go of someone you truly love. Because you invest so much time in that person. Or you may have a history with him. However, if it did not work, it is because 1. He was not meant for you 2. God has someone better for you 3. Right now, you guys need to be apart to grow and heal and then come back together again. There's a saying if you love him, let him go if he comes back then that's how you know. If he does not come back, the best man is on the route. But we must let go to know. There's a saying, "One man's trash is another man's treasure." One man's whore is another man's wife because that person sees value in you. All men are not the same. Some men are mentally strong enough to handle any and everything; some men are not. Every man has a weakness. It's how you treat a man's weakness to make it a strength. What you are craving takes time to build, depending on the person.

There's a motive behind every man's action; the same is true for a woman. At the end of the day, if you are the one, he will make you his one and only. If he is not into you, you will know. A man will entertain who he wants to entertain, whether it's you or his ex or you again or other women. You can curse, you can fight, you can break things, you can pop up at houses, make threats, make phone calls, slash tires, set his house on fire. He will still entertain whoever he feels is in his best interest. All you are doing is making a fool out of yourself by responding to his actions. You don't need to act out for a reaction or to show you are not to be played with. It may feel good now; however, it doesn't prove anything. Acting out of rage may be what was needed to get all that frustration out; however, how are you benefitting from it?

Ask yourself these questions: What will it cost you? Or benefit you? If it comes with a good purpose of purging, do what makes you happy. At the end of the day, what sense does it make to be left with the same hurt, and pain, or to jail? Love yourself enough to accept what was and move forward to what is. Go through the journey of healing yourself because there's a lesson in every situation. You can always prove yourself in a class, sassy way. You can kill him with silence and start changing up your ways. Move in silence—it's better that way—and start doing things he never would expect you to do such as changing your hair, going out more, dressing up more, hanging around business-minded or like-minded people, changing your number if needed, switching up your wardrobe. Learn to be versatile. I'm pretty sure it will have him questioning you and himself. Do it to better you. Turn that anger into something positive or towards something positive.

You will see the positive outcomes of your actions whether or not you still deserve him or if it is worth it, you can decide to take him back. If not, it's not worth it. Another man will come around and give you what you desire and love you how you want to be loved and treat you how God loves on His children that He cherishes. Don't waste your time and energy on a man that doesn't see any future with you as he reminds you of that. Remind yourself that your *true* husband is out there waiting on you to leave that pointless relationship. Love yourself and remember that your peace of mind is more important than being in an unhappy, toxic relationship. Be still and wait upon the Lord for He will give you the desires of your heart. Trust in Him. He is in control; just wait on Him.

MEN-Drunk-EN-Ness (His Story)

Ever been betrayed to the point your loyalty, love, and trust for the person was gone? I've dated many women, but their heart was not right. As a young boy, I watched my mom walk out on me and emotional betray me for sex and money. My dad transition when I was ten. I remember it was late October, I was in my room playing the game. My dad was walking out his room when he started coughing blood, he was trying to call my name and all I kept hearing him whisper son, son. I heard a hard collapse and when I rushed to the kitchen it was my dad lying on the ground choking on his blood. I screamed for help and called 9-1-1. When he reached the hospital, three hours later doctor said he was dead. After my dad's funeral, my uncle took me in as his own, still my mother betrayed me for sex and money. My uncle was an OG in the streets, selling heavy drugs and guns. He had people jealous and envious of how much money he made. Even though my uncle sold drugs, he always gave back to his community and made an impact by giving to any event to help the community grow. Because of this, his so-called friend was hating.

They set him up at his residential place. My uncle had two houses, the main and a place of business. I witness his death firsthand. He had a couple of chicks over and him and his so-called friends were playing domino's. They were in the guest room discussing their next move. They began to drink heavily and smoke, as they laughed and laughed and laughed. One of his friends said Fuck you, shot him in the face. All you heard were rounds and screaming. The girls ran out the house expect for his friends. They placed the gun in his hand, robbed him, and reported suicide. From there, all I had were father figures.

Back to my mom. She was supposed to be the role model of my life, the example of the woman I should married, but after she had done betrayed me. I look at all women differently. Betrayal is so hurtful that you become numb to the pain. You can't even look at the person the same anymore. I was also in love with a woman because she was different, gave me everything my mom couldn't give me. She understood my scar's. She spoke my love language. She was too perfect to be true. I played her a couple times in the past but my love for her was strong. Until one day, I found out she had a miscarriage. I went through her phone and found out she was dealing with another man. It started off with a small talk, drinks, and then led to one-night stand. She took my hard earnings to spend it on him.

Imagine, living with betrayal in your heart which is so hard to overcome because I once trusted her, and I was loyal to her; too loyal to her. I taught her loyalty because her family didn't. I was once in love, in love with a woman whom I trust. She was everything to me—my world, my peace, my joy—until she betrayed me. While I was holding onto a dream, she took everything within me. It cut so deep that I became wounded, and the wound joined my past scars and together they weighed heavily on me. I was also betrayed by the streets and frenemies, betrayed by the justice system that was made for men like me, betrayed by exes who were just a mind-relief, betrayed by my own reflection, and now by her.

How am I supposed to look at my reflection if she keeps reminding me of old scars? Didn't I show you loyalty?

When I did, I got shoved down. And I'm supposed to keep the peace! My ego was too strong to bow down to what I didn't know. I've been exposed to so much in these streets that I've became a victim, stereotyped, marginalized, and a statistic to society. Now, I am numb and desensitized to the world. My flesh is weak; the man in me is no longer me. There's a war within me. I am fighting between demons and God, so I drink to cover pain and to mute the voices I hear inside my head. Instead, the drinking releases the demons within me, and as expected most of them intoxicated further worsening my predicament. Now I am labeled as drunk, a wild boy, and seen as naked, aggressive, and living in a cold world – just in a rage. But my whole life wasn't staged. If I had never lived in the fast lane, my life would have had a different name. No, I'm not a drunk. I just need someone to help ease the past pain.

When I was young, I lived in the fast lane and lived a life with many names. I was played by these streets and gunned down by lame boys (slang word fake). My manhood was denied by the justice system, so I had no games to play, no freedom, no freedom of speech. I was robbed and cheated by them as I witness the system destroy my life into pieces as well as the lives of many others. The same energy I put into these streets wasn't returned to me. Instead, it came back with a letter from the courts saying, I was now yours, sentenced to prison, now sell your soul. The streets don't love you. It was a trap to make you a victim or take you to your early grave. The system is here to take your soul, the same way your right-hand man would with his eyes closed—deny you three times as Peter did to Jesus—betray you like Judas then take your life. The same person you watched grow or were in diapers with will take your soul and sell it to the devil for coins, just to have a name.

It will psychologically f*** you up because the hate is real, the jealousy is real, and the envy is real. It's so fucked up that your own family will trade on you just to watch you die while burying you alive, only to stand in front of your casket to share fake memories and shed fake tears, to put a R.I.P in front of your name. Now that

I'm gone, you want to water me and say long live these roses. Now I'm just a dead man walking miles in your thoughts. Now you notice me. When I was living you didn't even give two f**** about me. Where are my roses, don't want them at my funeral? Now that you have seen another side of me, now you can't compare. But the love was real, just from afar. Are my roses still growing or did they just fade away? How long before I'm forgotten? Tupac was right—but life goes on. Now the beast within is alive, what now? It is awake and feeding on the hurt and pain. I'm not a drunk, I'm just hurting. I have seen so many things, messing with these streets that PTSD became a part of me, a new identity. So, you thought only military men suffered from that. Believe it or not, men like me suffered from it too. When you grow up fast, you see, hear, and experience life early and now it becomes a part of you.

I'm just a man looking for peace within me. My insecurities got the best of me because of the hurt I was enduring. There was no one to say I see your pain, let me help. Instead, people continued to let me drown; only when they needed a handout did, they pull me in. It hurts. Hurt people hurt people. That's a true statement. I wanted revenge. I felt alone. I wanted everyone to feel every pain I felt. Therefore, I roared in drunkenness, anger, and in pain. This was a drunk man's cry. Why not help his tears dry? How else was I supposed to express pain when society teaches boys not to cry? Society plays a huge role in promoting men to be masculine, strong, powerful, and never to fail, or be weak or vulnerable. As a child society teaches boys to hide their fears.

When men become desensitized, we are labeled emotionless, and cold-hearted because we live our life guarded. We carry the weight of the world on our shoulders. Do you see the difficulties of being a man and trying to keep and obtain the ideal image and perception of what a man should be, internally and externally? If I pick up a drink once in a blue, do not judge me. Come wrap your arms around me and hold me. Society never taught us how to cry, manage our emotions, or cope with our external problems. It taught us to drink alcohol and smoke our problems away. Maybe, just maybe, tomorrow you'll wake up in an unknown place. Alcohol became my new peace while sex numbed my pain away. It was close enough to give me temporary peace. Well, the peace of mind I needed. Alcohol and sex became my enemies and my best friends, my resources for verbal writings when my heart needed to release and express how it felt. Every time I felt pain, I turned to sex and alcohol. I don't do drugs, but with a sober mind, I'll have you addicted to my pain too. Manipulating as I can be, I had women believing in me, enough to give my mind relief. They were my high when I needed them the most. They became my drugs and therapy. They were addicted to me. I couldn't leave them alone because my ego got the best of me.

See, my emotions lead me to be so vulnerable that they had the best of me, leading me into a rage where I couldn't think for myself because at those moments, I was too busy reliving the hurt and harboring the pain. Even when I was burying my feelings, unforgiveness, my past hurts, pain, anger, and worries crept up on me. All the signs were present but ignored. If my drunkenness overtook me because of what was bothering me, the feelings of the circumstances that were bottled in. My hidden emotions were getting the best of me and killing me slowly. Not one of my loved ones was willing to help me manage them or get me help. Instead, they continue to feed my soul.

Now, my words became my weapon, and my action became my flames. I never had the intention of taking my hurt and turning them into flames. If I acted out, it was out of emotions and pain. As a man, I am suppressed—suppressed by emotions, suppressed as a man, suppressed as a black man and as a minority, suppressed by the majority, suppressed by women, oppressed by the oppressor. I *am* a *great* man with a great heart who take care of loved ones. The woman I loved couldn't love me the way I loved her, couldn't be there for me as I would be for her, cater to me the way I would cater to her, run for me the way I would run for her, kiss my wounds the way I would kiss hers. All I wanted was a woman to come home to help me heal these wombs, to help me to restore myself, and to challenge *me to aspire for the best*. Instead, she pushed me away and made excuses as to why she couldn't do x, y, and z.

Therefore, I found someone who understood me and made my pain a little easy. So yeah, I took advantage of it. She was giving me what I needed and more. I held onto her because when the home wasn't right, she knew how to get me right at the right moment. It's like she was on time with time. No questions asked. In the back of my mind, I'm wishing why this wasn't your life, it would have been a better place for me. Momentary, she is my <u>right-now</u> lady. You had me entertaining someone I don't even see a future with, but if she continues, she might end up being your replacement. Right now, she is becoming your temporal substitute.

Our problem is I can't even come home to peace of mind without you fucking shit up. Instead, you bring out the worst of me. All I want to do is love you, but you are too blind to see it. All I asked from you is to handle me with care and you could not even do that. How can a man give you all of him and still you can't bear it? It wasn't easy to walk away from someone I love but I needed to get away. Every time I looked back; it came with a price. Yes, you had your moments when you put a smile on my face and there were times, I would have to ask for that smile. Why should I have to ask for a smile? I was tired, tired of being suppressed and oppressed. You just weren't ready for a man like me. Even while I was cheating on you, I still forced myself to make our relationship work because I loved you so much. I kept it honest with you, and yet you gave me pain. My love was real. I didn't want to lose or hurt you. How can you not see the love that I have for you? This is not the route I wanted to take with you. You disappointed me. Our relationship is not healthy. We are creating toxic air. We are disrespecting each other and calling each other names. You are creating the feeling of hate. You meant the world to me. How could you? Maybe you'll realize it. It's sad what we are going through has to be taught the hard way.

Hopefully, it is not too late for love to find its way again. The way I'm feeling, she may not be it for me. Little does she know; I'm confiding in other women too. And to answer your question—yeah, I cheated multiple times on you, but you only know of this one because she was consistent. She was there for me when you couldn't hear me. She was my peace when you couldn't be. My love for you will always remain. Just remember I was a good man to you. Don't make it seem as if I was a crafty man to you because I started to do you the way you did me. No, my actions weren't right, but how long can a man silently cry? Now, I'm on the battlefield trying to figure it out because I am confused. I'm sorry about this.

The way I feel, I don't think I want you, not right now. I'm starting to settle just because I feel contentment. You pushed me to the point where my loyalty doesn't lie within you anymore. I don't even look at you the same no more. The woman I once knew is no longer around because she died. I no longer want to do this anymore. So, for now, it's her and them. Let's just hope the one year of cheating on you doesn't turn into two years of loving someone who should have been you. At this point, she is treating me so right. Sorry, I don't even see us working out. Maybe in the future, when you get it right.

Unbeknownst to you, a drunk man's cry is a cry for help, a cry for change, and a cry of frustration. A cry of understanding, a hug, hearing "I love you and I miss you," getting a rub on the head while hearing "Baby, let me run your bath" or hearing "Everything will be alright." Maybe it's deeper than that. Maybe he's depressed and wants someone to hold him tight instead of bottling everything inside. I may be naked to you but I'm fully clothed.

Don't look at me half empty when I'm half full. I appreciate my weakness and my flaws even when my strength looks good within. It's deeper than this drunk man because the intention to hurt is still there. So please bear with me while I slowly heal from this pain you caused me. The least you can do is help me heal, but instead, you're burying me. Silence kills and drunkenness does too because only a foolish woman would do what you do.

CONVERSATION OF CONFESSIONS
(PART 2)

HE: I loved this woman like no other. I gave her my all. I never gave another woman my heart the way I gave it to her. What hurts the most is knowing that you kept hurting me, leading me to think you had my best interests at heart. I thought I had a true woman at home to love me and cared for me. When a man gives his heart to a woman, treasure it. I thought you would. There are always two sides to the story. Just know I was there for you and always be there. My loyalty to you was pure and after I felt betrayed and misled, my trust for you vanished. On another note, bae, I love you. I don't want to lose you. I'm killing myself, all choked up in my pain and the mess I've created. But *wait*! I didn't create this alone. Instead of helping me heal through this, you made me feel otherwise. Also, I was dealing with past hurts that I haven't overcome yet. The fact that I held you to a high standard with expectation, thinking you would be all that and more, killed me. Since someone else was doing what I expected of you without any questions, I held onto her. I wasn't being patient or waiting on God to continue to mold my future wife because I thought she was already complete.

Now, I don't know whether it's you or me. I am confused. I am stuck between the two, the past woman and my future woman. I deserved to be loved and handled correctly. The more you push me away the more she pulls me in. The more she fills the void, the more she makes me complete. Man, women are crazy in their way, but when I needed you, you gave up on me and played me. She stuck by my side even when I brought her hell. She took my hell and turned it into something different. Something that I was expecting from you. So, I took it as a sign from God- sending me the love of my life. I do apologize for my poor decisions and my selfish ways. I apologize for taking advantage of you and using it for my selfish gains. I owned up to the things I have done and put you through. Do know, I love you.

Right now, I am still between a rock and a shell. I need time to focus and figure this out and on myself and what I want. I can't give you the best of me when I can't see what's best for me. I have failed you many times and wasn't man enough to face my demons and heal from them. So, instead, I blamed you for them since you were the closest thing to me. And I allowed the pain to destroy the best part of me. I thought having multiple women would heal my pain, but instead, it created more demons within me and boosted my pride and ego. I felt I needed that because that's all I know. It's something about women that is so powerful. They know how to cater to a man when he is in the most vulnerable place, especially when they know the home is a mess. So, they step up to the plate and offer what we desire to the table. Yes, I was toxic in my ways, but I was craving attention, love, and affection. I wanted to feel and hear that I was appreciated – know that my presence as a man was needed. My soul craving increased the more. I've been under a lot of stress lately and it's killing me mentally and emotionally, even my health is on the line too. Honestly, I don't want to lose you and pray that our relationship restores to normalcy and bliss, soon. And to answer your question, I want to be your husband, and for you to be my wife.

Right now, I need time to find myself again because I've lost myself in years of pain. I do pray that God saves you for someone special, if it's not me. I want to go back to being the man who said, "Love is patient, love is kind. It does not envy, it does not boast, it is not proud. It does not dishonor others, it is not self-seeking, it is not easily angered, and it keeps no record of wrongs. Love does not delight in evil but rejoices with the truth. It always protects, always trusts, always hope, and always perseveres. Love never fails." Because it was deep to me, I was able to change into the man you once were in love with when I said those words, "When I was a child, I talked like a child, I thought like a child, I reasoned like a child. When I became a man, I put the ways of childhood behind me." I want to go back to who I was and be able to perform better so we can walk in faith, hope, and love. But keep vowing and keep voicing how you feel. Keep speaking until you can't speak anymore. When done, do not forget me. Let's heal together because *we* are in pain, we are dying, and together we can taste peace, joy, and happiness. I need peace! You need peace! We need peace! We both have a voice. We just don't know how to express it healthily because we operated in pain and misunderstand each other. Let's not kill the moment and work together to end our silent cry. Let's heal for a better mental, emotional, and physical spirit-man. I love you and together we will be strong. If things ever shift to where we do not ever get married, just know I will have a love for you, respectfully.

Quick Gem: A foolish man would miss out on a perfect woman because his barrel is full of options. But it takes a wise man to know which woman is a possession of prize. Sometimes, when a woman is willing to show effort and make a change. You can mold her to becoming a better individual and vs versa. It takes a real man to see that.

MAN'S SELF-ESTEEM

"The self-esteem of western women is founded on physical being (body mass index, youth, and beauty). This creates a tricky emphasis on image, but the internalized locus of self-worth saves lives. Western men are very different. In externalizing the source of their self-esteem, they surrender all emotional independence. (Conquest requires two parties, after all.) A man cannot feel like a man without a partner, corporation, and team. Manhood is a game played on the terrain of opposites. It thus follows that male sense of self disintegrates when the other is absent." - Antonella Gambotto-Burke, The Eclipse: A Memoir of Suicide

"Discipline is the most essential quality of the successful man. Discipline is your key to power, effectiveness, and freedom. A disciplined man can accomplish anything within the scope of his talents and abilities. An undisciplined man accomplishes nothing." - T.D. Jakes, He-Motions: Even Strong Men Struggle

"Face the giants in your life, slay them, and move on. Do not be daunted by the mistakes and failures in your life."-T.D. Jakes, He-Motions: Even Strong Men Struggle

A man's ego craves attention. He craves the attention that his mother probably didn't give him, or the world has downplayed to him. A man needs to be loved the same way we are loved. A man wants to expose his heart and weaknesses to you, but in a haven – meaning your lap has to be his safe place. It's good to learn his language, his love language, to love him properly while he is facing those demons within. A man needs someone to be genuine with him, to handle him with care, and speak to him in a tone that is not aggressive, not saying he always want a soft woman. We, as women, including me, need to find ways to appreciate a man, speak life to him, carter to him, love on him, pray for him, speak to him, not at him, and LISTEN to his needs. I believe with coaching, understanding, patience, and working with him through the process, the relationship will progress. Do not put an expectation on each other for it will cause a relationship to fail. As previously stated, a man needs to be heard, honored, cherished, empathized with, and reminded that he is loved. We need to boost his ego, meet his needs, help take the weight off his shoulders, surprise or take him out from time to time, make love to his mind and stimulate his soul. We need to make him feel like the King that he is and remind him he is a *king*, no matter what is presented in front of him. He is the superman that you see on television, the Clark Kent who has a weakness called kryptonite. Our men have kryptonite that they deal with and are faced with it every day, even when they try to hide it. When they can't be strong, help them build on it. We need to send him text messages, visit him at his job, whisper in his ears, flirt with him, speak life into him, and send him pictures. Men need prayers from when they wake up and to when they go down to sleep. Pray for them and pray with them. Be their reflections, not their affliction. Be a great representation of them in the house and the streets.

Men are hurting in silence, and no one is willing to hear them or heal their pain. They are dealing with depression, suppression, and oppression. That's why they say a strong man needs a strong woman. Instead, we, society, add to their pain and mistreat their ego. Men have so many responsibilities. They do so much to keep a smile on one's face. The hard work they put in does not amount to what we put even though it's their job. When in a relationship, it's important to not let everyone into your business because they will plant their values, beliefs, and morals in your relationship. What works for you doesn't work for everybody else. Yes, you should have one or two individuals you can confine that are willing to *listen* and *not project their life experiences onto you*. Just because women share similar stories doesn't mean situations will end the same. Men suffer so much in silence. When they are trying to be heard, we neglect them. We don't try to hear them. We just push them away. When we do hear them out, we play on it and mock them. We want them to be the superhero, but who will be theirs? We tend to forget the weight that is on their shoulders, and they can't depend on anyone to carry that weight. There's so much pressure on them along with attachments to insecurities. We should boost their ego. Men are like babies and toddlers, needing compliments, wanting to be pampered from time to time, cared for, understood, and convinced you are there for them.

    Men, you are a true gift from God the same way women are. Men, you are valuable defined as a temple, a sanctuary, a lion, a provider, a King. You hold a crown. You are the lions in the jungle, the ruler of your homes, kings, and the protectors of your families. Men, you are a captain of the ships that guide women through the ocean of life. When the waves hit, you know how to send signals to calm the storm. You are made in the likeness and image of God, a representation of God. You are a visionary, and an educator of your teachings. You are motivators, overachievers, self-educators, militants, soldiers, rulers, and leaders. Men, you are the power and the source of light/energy. You are majestic and a hero. Men, you are true hustlers, business-minded, purposeful, millionaires, and passionate lovers with talents, and gifts. Men, you are the protector, provider, visionary, and procreator—the seed supplier and the fertilizer.

Men, you are appreciated and loved. Men, we love you and appreciate all that you do even when it's not said enough. You have done so much for us such as being the provider, the protector, the teacher, and whatever hats your wear considering us women-making a home is in good standing and putting a smile on our faces. Women; men need us the same way we need them. Men are as important to us as we are to them. Men, I commend you. We, women, commend you for your hard work, your diligence, and the weight that you carry. I commend you for putting your best foot forward. You deserve more national days, not just Father's Day. As women, we need to protect your ego and make you feel loved and not belittled. We need to value your presence and value your character. Within the home, cooking a meal and some sex is not enough. We should be running your bubble baths, treating you when we go out, and doing the trivial things that count—maybe massaging your feet or giving a full aromatherapy massage. You don't ask for much, but to be loved and to be understood. You are strong because you suffered in silence for too long. That's why when you roar, you roar in rage or drunkenness. Ladies let's make every day special the same way men make it special for us.

Another tip for the men: Dr. Veronica G. Bee stated, "By nature, men are givers and women are receivers. Women take and men give, so then women are taken what is given to them and give it back multiplied whether it be good or bad. Men, whatever you are giving out, she will receive it and give it right back to you in greater measure (Why Women Act Foolish, 2019)." That right there is enormously powerful. Whatever seed you plant in a woman during the relationship is what she will give back to you in multiple ways. Watch how you manage her heart and her mind. Men must learn to handle the issue and not act deranged or send threats about killing her if she dates someone else, or you feel you have to fight her and her man because she cheated or left you. Life would be better if you can deal with the situation rationally without being in your feelings. Irrational thinking can cause jail time or the taking of someone else's life due to you not knowing the right way to handle a situation. If you can't handle it, don't get into a relationship until you know how to communicate. It goes vice versa. For my men, think of it this way: be glad, she did, or you did. Let another person deal with that craziness. We have all invested in someone; we all took risks. What did we learn from it? How did the relationship better you? How did it bring clarity to what you do want, or do not want? What will be different the next time? Do you even care what type or kind of women you attract? What will she bring to the table to create the foundation you want? Is she like-minded? Can you guys connect on a spiritual or on any kind of level? Does she represent you? This question goes for women as well. The same rules apply to you when mastering yourself.

Fellas, know your worth, know yourself enough to know not to tolerate the bullshit from people. Love yourself enough to where no one can devalue your character. Don't let any man or woman cause you to feel less than or degraded. Don't let anyone make you feel you are a product of where you came from. Embrace your background and childhood. They created who you are and will be tomorrow. You are one of a kind and should be appreciated, loved, and honored for the work that you do. You should never feel defeated or let another man intimidate you based on what he didn't work hard for or based on his success. Everyone has their season to grow and shine, and when it is your turn, *shine harder*. Fellas, you are amazing, intelligent, aggressive when needed and *a man*. Let no one define who you are as a *man*. You are *you* for a reason whether other people agree or not. Men, we love you!

On another note, men, after you heal yourself and know who you are, you will be able to find your favorites, your helpmate that was specifically ordained and designed for you. Remember you are the leaders, the head of the household. When you step into your position and take your role in Christ, you will love your wife as Christ loves the church, which means you will be faithful to her and not cheat, be gentle, and have self-control. You will know how to manage your family and operate in respect and love, so your children can obey and follow your commands. When you walk in obedience to God and hear from Him – the foundation that God is building/creating will be ordered by Him. This also teaches our future children the character of God and a sense of direction.

Quick Gem for the Men and Women: Stop looking for and accepting convenient love, when we deserve REAL LOVE!!!! Not that condition love, that unconditional love. Not that love that comes with terms and conditions, but love that it unlimited. We are to deserving to be sleeping next to a man or a woman who are temporary or just momentary. You are not a conveniency or a convenient store. Stop treating yourself as such. The word convenient means fitting well with a person's needs, activities, and plans (https://www.merriam-webster.com/).. meaning **suitable, handy useful, advantageous**. Why would you want to fit someone's needs or plans, or be useful, handy, or suitable when it is best fitting for them?! Sounds like an option. When I need you, I can call on you. Whenever wherever and you will be fine with it. We are better than that. We are more than options. Why would you want to sleep at night with tears crying knowing that he or she is cheating on you, disrespecting you, walking out on you and choices when he or she wants to enter your life? Why would you want to settle with a man or a woman who cannot commit to you and give you what he or she truly deserves of you and for themselves? Through experience, I rather sleep alone knowing that I am stress free, drama free, worry free, knowing on the other side, there is a real person wanting to love you and me vs waking up to a person who brings and give you and me anxiety, stress, drama, sex that is probably not adventurous. I rather an individual that I can built with, speak life over me, love me unconditionally without any terms and conditions, that I can have access too without the fear of another individual has that same access to his or her heart. I rather wake up thanking God for this amazing soul lying next to me vs praying God to change this individual when they are not ready or willing to change. I rather come home to an individual knowing they will be there waiting to be loved on vs questioning will they be there when I arrive or before I go to bed. **So, what if he or she gives you money or gave you something that you were missing that the last person couldn't give you or you could not have given yourself.** There's someone out there that can give YOU BETTER. You are praying that Ciara's or Russell's prayer or want that prayer but not willing to walk away from that broken toxic individual. That person needs healing themselves. You can always have more and better. You have to want it, and first, find it within you. Stop settling for convenient love and give yourself that unconditional love. Choose wisely what you want and deserve. Save yourself from the drama, the depression, the tears, the headache, the hurt, the pain, the insecurity, the mistrust, the lies, the cheating, the betrayal, the abandonment, the abused, the manipulations, the taking advantage of, the heartbreak, and everything that is toxic.... Unless that what you want ....

We all are searching and needing love on another level. Our body, mind, and soul are looking for that right love, hungry for love and someone's presence, praying and seeking for that love. Looking for love on all types and kind of level. Search for that real love, that love God speaks of, his love that endures forever, that agape love, unconditional love, that no matter what love. Learn to put God first then yourself. Set your heart free from all the toxic things. Search for someone who can commit, satisfy your body, mind, and soul, who studied your character, know when to make you smile, leave you alone when you need to cool off, knows how to love, caress your soul, faithful, affectionate, compassionate, gentle, great listener, careful, good intentions, patient, consistent, persistent, being able to submit, understanding, loyal, secure, someone you can be yourself around, knows how to sacrifice, gives you reassurance… Whatever it is may mean for you. It may not be all of that I have listed. It can be simple and that is fine. Most women and men do not ask for much. As long as it represents what you are looking for and it is given within their measure. Unless they are willing to give more and stretch above and beyond, effortlessly.

THE PLANET OF A FOOLISH WOMAN

A foolish woman is a double-minded woman. She operates in that Jezebel spirit and willing to stay that way. The Jezebel spirit is always controlling, operating in the authority, manipulating, and wanting to dominate things. They always have deep, unhealed wounds from sources such as rejection, resistance, fear, insecurity, self-preservation, and bitterness, which in turn, spreads its defilement to many. Lastly, they are influenced by their pride, independence, and rebellion. She is willing to act petty and act like a child although she's a whole grown adult; the same goes for a man. A foolish woman has a cold heart and can't build a positive relationship with her spouse, family members, or friends because of what she has in her heart. She is stuck in her ways and not willing to renew her mind. She doesn't know how to bring peace into her world or her man's world. Her tongue is uncontrollable. She knows how to tear a man and a woman down with her word, like a weapon. She does not see the big picture because she is all about self and myopic toward positivity.

She can also carry the spirit of Miss. Independent; I do not need a man. She can be the woman that always wants to monitor everything that is going on. She wants things to operate her or no way. A foolish woman does not take counsel or correction easily. She can't even take the word of wisdom from the wise because she operates in carnality and closed-mindedness. She cannot see change and does not want to change. She hurts people and thinks everyone is against her. She cannot see the man God brought to her because she operates in the division and is disconnected from God's purpose. One thing is when God blesses you with a good man, if you do not treat him accordingly someone else will. He will move on while you are trying to figure out what he did wrong when the question is what you did wrong.

A foolish woman would assume and create storylines in her head, living in her mind, thinking of situations that are not true. A foolish woman would believe in the lies people tell and react to a situation that is not present. She wears her full armor ready to war (meaning she has a guard up ready to fight, attack, or clap back) with people, even her future husband-to-be or husband. She would come home and complain out of expectation about a man, who cannot measure up to the assignment. The home is not peaceful because drama is written all over it. She cannot receive good counsel because she is always right or too stubborn to want to change. She rather is stuck in her ways verse comprising to make both parties happy.

Proverb 14 :1 says, "Every wise woman builds her house, but the foolish one tears it down with her own hands." (WEB). A woman trying to be the man when God created a man to be the head and the woman to follow is a result of misplaced priorities. She doesn't know her place as a woman. In Pastor Scott L. Harris's sermon, he described "the levels of a foolish woman and where she stands":

1. "The first is *kesîl* (kes-eel') which describes those who are dull and obstinate in their proclivity to make wrong choices. Among the behaviors and characteristics described in Proverbs by this word are hating knowledge (1:22), being complacent (1:32), displaying dishonor (3:35), spreading slander (10:18), being arrogant and careless (14:16), being without sense (17:16), revealing

their mind instead of delighting in understanding (18:2), can be perverse in speech (19:1), and consume their resources up (21:20). Because of these various traits, they proclaim folly to others (12:23) and display it in how they live (13:16), so they will suffer harm (13:20). A boisterous woman is this kind of fool that is naive, ignorant, and gullible (19:13).

2. The next level of foolishness is *ewil (eh-wil)* or *iwwelet (iw-weh'-let)* meaning "thick" "thick-brained" and "stupid," denoting a person that is morally deficient lacking in sense, and being generally corrupt. Among the behaviors and characteristics described in Proverbs by this word are despising wisdom and instruction (1:7), lack of understanding (10:21), being right in their own eyes (12:15), quick-tempered (14:17), deceitful (14:8), rejecting discipline (15:5), lacking sense (15:21), speaks before listening (18:13), rages against the Lord (19:3), quarreling (20:3) and stubborn (27:22). These characteristics will lead to their ruin by their own words and actions (10:10, 14) for they proclaim folly and display it in how they live (12:23; 13:16). A woman who has this type of foolishness destroys her own home by her own hands (14:1)." (Harris. P. (2016, May 08) The Wise Woman vs the Foolish Female. Retrieved from (gracebibleny.org)

I HAVE A VOICE TOO

Submissive: ready to conform to the authority or will of others; meekly obedient or passive.

Submission: the action or fact of accepting or yielding to a superior force or the will or authority of another person.

Miss. Independent is what I call her. She doesn't need a man because she has her own. Yes, she got her own –her car, home, money, and a 9-5 job with a little side hustle. So, a man cannot control her. She's been TAKING CARE of herself and her home for many years. Independent enough to take herself on luxury vacations and eat at fine restaurants. No man knows how to address her because she is too independent. So, don't dare tell her what to do. She controls her world, what she thinks, eats, and acts; her when, where, and how. Therefore, don't you come here trying to interrupt her and her peace. What she says goes and she is never wrong. She does not submit unless she feels like it. If you don't cater to her needs, forget yours. Let me tell you a story: One day, he came home trying to make demands and I was not willing to listen. While I was talking, the very word that would spark an argument and a fight - came out with aggression - SHUT UP!! I froze! How dare he tells me to shut up? Who the Hell does he think he is? After that, my mouth became a weapon.

Who does he think he is making demands? Just because society makes it alright for him to disrespect a woman does not mean he does. Don't play by the rules; be the rules. No, I'm not being rude or coming in a form of a feminist. I'm just giving you a piece of advice. He didn't know I was a strong-minded, dominant woman, who came from strong-minded parents. My parents were so domineering, it was like having two male lions running the jungle. I also think it's in my genes. See, the women in my family are strong-minded as well. They do not take shit from anybody, not even their men.

Here's a perfect example, my mom does not allow my dad to run her, and she put her foot down when things didn't go her way or when my dad was demanding too much. My aunts on my dad's side are very domineering and religious. You couldn't tell them to go left if they felt in their spirits to go right. So please, you can't run me. I've been independent for twenty years. I respect and love you, but my ways, you can't avoid. No, I'm not better than you. I'm just enlightening you. I feel, as a woman, that a man should understand a woman can express herself too. Of course, we, as women, do love to complain about this and that. It is in our nature, right?

Why do men think women don't have a voice too? This is not back-in-the-day, ancient times when women had to stay silent. Based on biblical laws, people say a woman must submit to her man. Nothing wrong with that, but no man is about to make me his slave. I'm not the shut-up type and never will be. I can't shut up. My voice is too precious. Don't get upset with me for feeling how I'm feeling. I'm a woman; I'm supposed to express myself. I'm only human, sheesh. He wants me to shut up in public but speak only in the bedroom. He has me all messed up.

When was the last time you shut up when a man told you to? You better not be a coward and show him. See, in a relationship, men think they can run you and everything that comes with it. There are times when you want to remind him who wears the pants. That will make him feel so uncomfortable. It's like you just rob him of his manhood. Some men speak to women as if they are their children. No sir, I'm not your child; I'm your woman. Treat me accordingly. You won't make me feel less of a woman or powerless. So, yes, I can speak. I have a voice too. Nothing that he says can change how I feel because my feelings will never fail me. Foolish I am, foolish I will be. I won't let anybody control me or say anything that will make them feel less superior.

GEM 101: THE LESSON

For the strong-minded woman, it doesn't mean she can't be submissive, passive, or assertive. At times, a strong-minded individual plays a role of a strong woman because she is strong-minded or is not a yes woman. She speaks what she feels is right and there's nothing wrong with standing strong and having a voice. At the end of it all, our strong personality creates challenges and problems for those who view us as always being right or wanting to be in control of things. At times, people miss out on the big picture and override what's really going on because they see a strong, independent, controlling woman.

I believe we can become submissive and assertive, but a few choose not to. Some tend to think what they say goes and that's all—like they are the dominant ones in the relationship. I believe a foolish woman can sometimes be a dominant woman who doesn't want a man to lead her or because she has been hurt in the past. There's nothing wrong with taking a step back and stepping into the role of being submissive and assertive. Yes, somewhere along the line, the authority role came into the play when someone mistreated us or instill that mindset within us; it can be generational. If you don't want to be single for the rest of your life, you need to take ten steps back.

A foolish woman would allow her home to break down and do nothing to save it. She would allow her man to drown and not save him. A foolish woman can't find ways to save anything because she thinks only of herself. She can't tell the difference between genuine love and fake love. She is so nearsighted that she becomes blindsided. What you get is what you put into it. She can display behaviors of being passive-aggressive, manipulative, and or indirect. A foolish woman carrying her pride of Miss. Independent and not willing to let her guard down. Don´t be a foolish woman. Be wise in everything that you do because a wise woman keeps her home and knows the right timing of everything to keep her man and home happy. Dr. Juanita Bynum said, "You have a responsibility to make our husband feel like a wonder man even when you know he is not. Don't focus on what he is not- and make him feel amazing. Don't remind him of his past or what he doesn't do or someone else will make him feel like a man. Submission means I find his vision and I put myself in the position to always keep him on time. It takes two to make a relationship/marriage go bad. What did you learn from your past relationship? Don't let a man play clean up. There are going to be areas in your mate's life that he is never going to be healed from. There are going to be things, certain things you can't touch because they are too sensitive" (Marriage Sermon Other. 14.March 2015. *Proverb 31 Women Be a Wife Juanita Bynum.* [Video File] (YouTube Channel) https://www.youtube.com/watch?v=NkKzIpF1MMI&t=9s. A man doesn't ask for much—just to be loved and someone to have his back.

We, as women, have a problem—we feel we should have the last word. At times, we need to learn to shut up. Our mouths are deadly weapons; we can cause people and things to die. We can kill a man's self-esteem and make him feel worthless instead of uplifting him. We place so much expectation on our men, knowing they cannot fulfill it to our capacity, only to the measure of his capacity.

Quick Gem: A man can also be foolish as well and tear down his home with lies and cheating, stepping out of his role as the man and the head of the household, failing his family, and not doing what he is supposed to. Speaking against his wife and not being aligned. In the bible, Amos 3:3 says, "Do two walks together, unless they have agreed," (WEB).

THE PLANET OF A WISE WO-MAN

"Wisdom comes from experience, the knowledge of understanding what you are going through is the gateway to the next level, opportunity, and/or open door. A wise woman creates her atmosphere and set the tone/ foundation of her household. A wise woman knows who she is, because of her identity in God. She is noble and business-minded as a boss, she does not play or tolerate drama or negativity. She is all about wealth because her legacy is for her family. A wise woman needs the wisdom to create a wealthy mindset, so she and others attached to her purpose can endure. The way God works is wisdom feeds into knowledge that will attract all that we need, like the tools to be that woman God destined us to be."

– Cassandra Edouard

Proverbs 12:4 says, *"A worthy woman is the crown of her husband, but a disgraceful wife is as rottenness in his bones."* (WEB). At the time of writing this book, I couldn't write from the perspective of a wise woman because I was a foolish woman tearing down her own home. Because I was operating in hurt, I was the damaged and hurt woman. I also had areas in my life that needed improvement. I was not seeing the grand prize of having a good man in the house. My pride was in the way of things. I thought I was Ms. Independent who could handle her own. I mean, I am not boasting; it is confidence. However, there is nothing wrong with having a great man to make things work. After doing some research, I have found some examples that I can foresee myself practicing in becoming a wise woman, a virtuous woman.

A wise woman doesn't mean only submitting to a man. It means submitting to God and herself. Here are some great examples of what I believe a wise woman is and hopefully these help as a guide for you to practice. A wise woman is defined as virtuous, faithful, good, hardworking, business savvy, provider for her family (cooking and serving), early riser, strength, well-rounded, enduring, charitable, trustworthy, a wife, and healthy (physical, mental, and spiritual), serving, honorable, mothered, wise, active, praiseworthy, excelling, god-fearing, rewarding, and a good steward. A wise woman is not defined as perfect however to live a purposeful life, a wise woman explores options, knowing that her man has a great intention to do something strong. She trusts a man's decision by first allowing him to be the man that he was created and destined to be.

A wise woman is willing to renew her mind and make a positive change within herself in order to build her future. A wise woman is willing to accept and take instruction from her wise man who is willing to counsel and submit to her when needed. A wise woman submits to her man in a way of giving him the power of being and feeling like a man. A wise man is willing to commit himself more to prove his love for the wise woman. A wise woman would not let a foolish woman tear down her home because she would not have flaws to avail the evil woman access to her home. A wise woman is single-minded. Proverb 14:1 says, "Every wise woman builds her house, but the foolish one tears it down with her own hands." (WEB). A woman who builds her house brings in great treasure. When a woman thinks of the word submission, she may define it to be letting the man take control of her life or every move. The word, "submit," means letting the man feel like the head and not the tail and allowing him to feel heard when the world or other people make him feel unheard. Submitting to him is not only going a day without complaining or nagging so much about things but also speaking in a polite, and passive way. A wise woman holding her tongue doesn't mean she is bowing down to a man. She can make a demand in a sexy way without him feeling she's coming at him. A wise woman knows what he likes and keeps it tasteful and classy.

I was reading a blog, *10 Traits of a Wise Women*, by Tracey Brewer (2015) explaining what makes a wise woman, according to her understanding of reading the bible. What I love about the blog is how she defines the character of a wise woman and their decision-making, how they carry themselves, and their level of faith, trust, and acts of obedience. Not only did this help me study the posture of a wise woman, but it also taught me through my own understanding of how I should be as a woman and a future wife. I love to share this part with you even though this is a biblical definition of a wise woman. However, this also shows us what a man loves, a balanced and mentally stable woman, a woman who can speak wisdom and be his haven in times of trouble. Not only that but a wise woman seeks wisdom, instructions, and revelations.

Here are the traits of a wise woman:

1. She fears the Lord. The Bible is direct in letting us know that this is the place to begin our quest for wisdom. *"The fear of the Lord is the beginning of knowledge: but fools despise wisdom and instruction."* (Proverbs 1:7 NIV)

2. She is teachable. *"Hear instruction, and be wise, and refuse it not"* (Proverbs 8:33 KJV). *"Give instruction to a wise man, and he will be yet wiser: teach a just man, and he will increase in learning"* (Proverbs 9:9 KJV). Whether learning from God's Word in our personal study or pastors

or Bible teachers or fellow Christians, a wise woman absorbs biblical knowledge and applies it to her life.

3. She controls her mouth. She talks less. *"In the multitude of words there wanteth not sin: but he that refraineth his lips is wise"* (Proverbs 10:19 KJV). A wise woman also uses her speech to be profitable and for our words to build up and encourage others. *"The tongue of the wise useth knowledge aright: but the mouth of fools poureth out foolishness"* (Proverbs 15:2 KJV).

4. She plans ahead. *"He that gathereth in summer is a wise son: but he that sleepeth in harvest is a son that causeth shame"* (Proverbs 10:5 KJV). Several verses in Proverbs 31 describe the virtuous woman as one who is organized and prepared.

5. She is careful in her choice of friends. *"He that walketh with wise men shall be wise: but a companion of fools shall be destroyed"* (Proverbs 13:20 KJV).

6. She fears the pull of sin and stays away from it. *"A wise man feareth, and departeth from evil: but the fool rageth, and is confident"* (Proverbs 14:16 KJV). A wise woman wants to recognize her weaknesses and keep herself out of situations that might provide temptation.

7. She seeks the counsel of wise people. When she doesn't know how to handle a certain situation, she should seek the Lord in prayer and then, as appropriate, seek advice from those she knows are wise. *"A wise man will hear and will increase learning; and a man of understanding shall attain unto wise counsels"* (Proverbs 1:5 KJV). *"The way of a fool*

is right in his own eyes: but he that hearkeneth unto counsel is wise" (Proverbs 12:15 KJV).

8. She guides her heart. *"Hear thou, my son, and be wise, and guide thine heart in the way"* (Proverbs 23:19 KJV). A wise woman guards her affections. She monitors her activities so that she has time for the things of the Lord and is not focused only on things of the world. It is wise for us as women to set guidelines to keep worldliness from slipping into our personal lives or homes.

9. She considers her latter end. *"O that they were wise, that they understood this, that they would consider their latter end!"* (Deuteronomy 32:29 KJV). This passage is talking about the children of Israel, but I think it can certainly apply to us women. We need to examine the many choices we make—whether small, daily, or bigger, potentially life-changing ones—and consider how they will impact our future here and in eternity.

10. She knows that all that happens in her life is in God's hands. *"For all this, I considered in my heart even to declare all this, that the righteous, and the wise, and their works, are in the hand of God"* (Ecclesiastes 9:1a KJV). From Solomon, the wisest man that ever lived comes this reminder that every event in our life is under God's control. (Tracey. 2015.www.girlstogrow.com/2015/06/10-traits-of-wise-woman.html)

After reading this, I realized the foolish woman I am because I cannot control my mouth, which implies I am in a defensive mood, so I am not teachable, and I tend to take matters into my own hands instead of knowing that all that happens in my life is in God's hands. I was not submitting to God, because I did not love God the way I should. I could not love the man he had for me.

[March 10, 2022, at 9:35 am in my thoughts: inspired from - Prayer Upper Room Intercession: Power of the Household by a wise prophet]

I never understood what it meant to be a wise woman because I was operating from a foolish place. The day I received clarity was when I was in a clubhouse, listening to the prophet. What I have learned from the series Power of the Household is that as wives, we must learn to be and stay in position. We must learn to understand our role, BUT to understand and know our role, we must first, submit to God. When we submit to God, we will know how to submit to our family and husband. Even though God called the man to be the head, we are the overseers of the family as a wife and woman. Our job is to make sure our family and husband are aligned, are clothed, are fed, and doing what it is they are supposed to, basically keeping the family and husband together. If we are not together, we cannot keep the family together, like a thread that holds things together.

To be a wise woman, you must learn to control your tongue and watch your mouth. Our mouth speaks of life and death because it has power. With that same mouth, we can bless or curse - that same mouth can cause your family to thrive or drown. We must ask God for more wisdom and counsel, whatever we say or do must be ordained by Him- ordered by Him. We can't speak from a place of hurt or pain, emotion, or live in our minds because it will cause us to destroy the foundation that God is building within us or around us. We cannot pray to become a wife and destroy our position that God is elevating and evolving us to be. Secondly, we must be healed from our past and allow God to shake, burn, and remove that very thing from our life. It's like going through the refinery, the silvering. The process is not easy, but the result is rewarding. When we pray for healing, we must understand that healing won't look like how we expect it to be. When God is healing us, He will remove and strip us from everything and everyone – to repair and renew what once was. God is creative, very creative. What he does sometimes, is that he will cause that very thing or person that hurt you to be present, to see if you really what to be healed. If you can withstand the areas, He is healing you from.

When God is preparing you to be a wise woman, to be a virtuous woman, processing you as a wife, you must first know how to submit to God, communicate with God, and have an intimate relationship with God to hear from Him and walk in obedience. This will lead women, (the wife) to be better servers and leaders, as well as fruitful to the family. We must lead by example so our children or future children can follow and your family and their family and generations to come will be a generation of blessings. When the women, take their rightful places and stay in position, it will lead the men to stay and play their role. As they are the head of the house, it will teach him to be faithful to God and his wife, great leader, exercise temperance- self-control, be no violent, manage his home and family, be gentle, and operate in and with respect so the children can obey and respect both parents. Lastly, when a virtuous woman, operates in the spirit of God, it teaches her temperance, peace, joy, love, counsel, and how to receive instruction and guidance from God to manage her family and children.

As wives or some to be wives, we must be mindful of who we share our business with, your trials concerning your marriage, relationships, courting, or family. The number thing we do is run to family, friends, and co-workers about what we are going through or facing, at this present moment. Instead of praying about the situation and consulting with God first. If we are not careful, those very words that you think are words of wisdom can be words of destruction. If it's not coming from someone with Godly counsel, not someone who will impose their values or judgment on you, you do not or should not speak, discuss, or mention it to them. They can cause that very thing that God put together to be cursed and torn apart. If you cannot pray about it, seek counseling. For most of us, this is the reason our relationship ended, is going through a rough patch, are divorced, or have family separated due to worldly advice. Worldly advice means- perspective through their lens, experiences, or relating it to the affairs of life or social aspects. How many of us can attest, testify, or agree that we allowed, or are the reasoning behind our destruction? So, we must be careful, not to allow anyone or everyone in your business.

Thirdly, the prophet stated that the way you treat God is the way you will treat your husband and your family. If you cannot communicate with God, you won't know how to communicate with your husband. Your relationship with God will be better, of course, however, he will counsel you on how to approach a situation because of the relationship you have with him. It teaches your children and husband how to handle life and its situation because they will say "I watched mom or my wife do x, y, and z." We are not perfect; however, it will teach us humility.

Fourthly, I learned from my parents the importance of having a relationship with God. They taught me about God. As a wife or a mother, you are the lead example and have to lead by example because your children (if you have) or husband is watching you. You are teaching them how to handle and manage life circumstances and who to run to when you are going through. Depending on your spirituality to get you through.

To my single ladies, it is better to be alone than be in a relationship and still feel single, unloved, unwanted, used and abused, lied to, or be a convenience. From experiences, I wanted to be loved and wanted to love someone, but that individual no longer felt the same for me. I was compared to other women, and when it came to sex or pleasing him. I was never fulfilling his needs. Deep down inside, I knew it was better to be alone than to be with a man who no longer feels the same way for me. I no longer have my best interest at heart. In his eyes, I was only a convenience to him. When he needed a temporary peace, he knew who to come to or if any of his other side chicks, were available to meet his needs. I was only a call away because I made myself available due to attachment, soul ties, and wanting him to love me back and prove I am here no matter what. The only thing I was doing, was hurting myself more and more. I wanted out, and when I did, I found myself going back because I was holding onto a prophecy (that this man was God-ordained. I was confused too how and why? I just did not understand how God can give me a man, who hurt me so bad. Not understanding the transition).

One day, he called to come over and I accepted. As I started to please him, I found myself compromising to please him. While I was robbing myself of affections, conversation, consistency, commitment, genuine love, and a kiss on the forehead, I was saying to myself that everything is going to be okay. All I was asking was for him to love me the way he did when we first met. As I was doing this, all I was doing was creating more open wounds and avoiding the red flags, because all I wanted was him; his presence. He was still opening the door for the other woman to still be in his life, to love her, take her out, receive those text messages, wake up to each other – giving the other woman a reason for him to keep her and appreciate her more – While I was the option when things do not go right. I was abusing myself because I refused to let him go. In my mind, if I stuck around, he would realize how much I love and want to be here for him. In this case, that did not change. No matter how many times he came over. No matter how much I cried and pray that was not bringing him back. My heart became heavy. I started bleeding inside wondering why and wishing this was not happening to me. Because I had an assignment/calling in my life, God had better plans. However, in my carnal self, I wanted him to be a part of the plan and be around. After seeing a picture of another woman, I saw my life flash in front of me, saying this is the end. As tears roll down my face. My heart became heavy, saying God thank you, but at the same time, thinking I thought we still had a spark. God, I thought you said this was the man ordained for me. How can this be? She is pretty, I am not going to hate her, but that should have been me.

What I did not know was God was ripping me apart from that relationship so I can build a better relationship with Him. God wanted to mold me and process me to become the woman he wants me to be and prepare me to be the wife I was destined to be. In the process, I was still questioning God and asking why? Because it came from a place of hurt and pain. That is why we need to be patient with God. I was not patient, because I thought by giving myself to him and being there for him; would bring him back- keep him around and willing to stay. It did not. It gave him a reason to put me back in that same place of trauma, hurt, and pain. I had to learn to reverse and give that position to God, submit to God, and trust that the ordained man for my life – has better benefits and package. I won't have to comprise, settle, and be taken advantage of. That feeling of void and rejection- being broken is not a safe place to be, but that broken place is to mold us to be a better version of ourselves. Like the song, gracefully broken. That broken place will make you appreciate and love who God has for you and love yourself and more.

It is in that broken place you evolve as a woman, the woman you always desire to be. It is in that broken place; you understand that Ciara prayer and create our own prayer. It is in that broken place; you can see the hands of God and His heart. If we lack wisdom, how can we overcome or prosper? So, we go through the storms, knowing that what we are experiencing, and with the wisdom and knowledge of God, we shall overcome, however, we must first believe it. The gift he had promised you and the gifts and talents hidden inside of you. It is in that broken place; you will see the wealth and glory of God manifest in your life. Be patient, prepare, and love yourself until God releases that ordained man for you. He is praying for you, covering you, and asking God when you guys will meet. In his patient, he is working on himself, he is not confused or cheating, neither is he causing drama, but just pacing himself to meet you.

Tip: I will never forget the fact that my mom would get upset, out of frustration and would say not-so-nice things because of her temper. We as mothers must watch what we say because it will come to pass, to fruition, and see it happen. Life and death are in our tongues. Our children can cause frustration even our spouses, but the power of prayer changes things. Instead of speaking about the things they have done, speak about the things that they will get done, reverse the curse, and reframe the negative. Instead of telling your child "You're so rebellious" say "I pray you start listening" or "I see you are going against what I am saying, just know not following instructions won't get you far." Instead of saying, "You are going to be like your father, who ended up incarcerated, selling drugs, and failing school" say "The path that you are taking is not a good path, I see a better future, be a change in the family to break patterning's." Instead of calling our children, "You're stupid or dumb" say "That was not smart or not a smart decision, you are wiser than I thought you were." Speak to the individual, not at them. Speak life and not curses.

Yes, the facts are in our face, but God gave us power and authority to speak against what we see. If the situation is frustrating you and eating you up inside, pray about it and do not say a word. James 1:19-20 WEB says, *"So, then, my beloved brothers, let every man be swift to hear, slow to speak, and slow to anger;* [20] *for the anger of man doesn't produce the righteousness of God."* Proverbs 15:1 WEB says, *"A gentle answer turns away wrath, but a harsh word stirs up anger."* Ephesians 4:29 ESV says, *"Let no corrupting talk come out of your mouths, but only such as is good for building up, as fits the occasion, that it may give grace to those who hear."* Ephesians 4:26 WEB says, *"In your anger do not sin"*[a]*: Do not let the sun go down while you are still angry.."* Luke6:45 WEB says, *"The good man out of the good treasure of his heart brings out that which is good, and the evil man out of the evil treasure of his heart brings out that which is evil, for out of the abundance of the heart, his mouth speaks."* These scriptures basically is telling us how to manage our mouth and behavior, and the kind of heart we should produce because out of your heart speaks how you truly feel and views the world and circumstance around you. For example, a petty person will reveal what is in their heart because they speak out of their mouth petty respond. A dramatic person will reveal what is in their heart because they will speak about gossip and problems, judgments instead of solutions, healing, and positivity.

FEAR OF REJECTION

"How One Rejection Can Change Your Life? Don't let the fear of rejection keep you out of the game. When you begin to realize that you're past does not necessarily dictate the outcome of your future, then you can release the hurt. It is impossible to inhale new air until you exhale the old."

— T.D. Jakes

Rejection: is the dismissing or refusing of a proposal, idea, etc. Synonyms: refusal, non-acceptance, declining, turning down, no, dismissal, spurning, rebuff repudiation, rebuff, spurning, abandonment, forsaking, desertion, shutting out, exclusion, shunning, cold-shouldering, ostracizing, ostracism, blackballing, blacklisting, avoidance, ignoring, snubbing, snub, cutting dead.

Rejection is a powerful feeling to experience outside of fear. It causes emotional and psychological distress which turns into pain. The thought of being rejected by others or loved ones can be detrimental to the soul. Rejection will have you feeling depressed, lonely, and worthless. Rejection will make you feel less than or have you thinking that you will never amount to anything- or have someone worthy enough to love for who you are or you can't receive the love because you feel you are not good enough. Rejection will have you afraid of the unknown, or not knowing what's on the other side- stopping the blessings God has for you, rejecting self, and self-sabotaging. Rejection will have you feeling as if you are not fit or qualified. Rejection will have you taking what people say or do personally and feeling defensive and quoting Bible scripture like "Guard your heart!" at all times. It was hard to cope with rejection, especially when the root of the problem may have come from close family, extended family, loved ones, friends, strangers, church members, work, etc.

As a child was always said NO when it came to going outside, attending events, or anything not related to church. I grew up fearing the word NO. I gave up. If I tried the first time. I wouldn't give myself the opportunity to try again. Living in a Haitian household, as a child, you have no voice. It is considered rude or fresh for a child to voice how they feel. You'll get smacked in the face, backhanded style if you were to think of expressing or voicing how you feel to your parents. It's best not to say a word. If you did, it was ignored. You were required to be silent and remain that way. Myra's mother did not play. She had such a strong personality. She could use words in a manner that cuts deep into your soul. They cut so deep you wished you weren't born. She felt her mom never acknowledged how she felt. When she cried and expressed her hurt, it was labeled as showing off or being dramatic. Myra's mother just wasn't trying to hear anything or was too busy and less focused on Myra. Nothing she said to her mother mattered. After a while, she just started internalizing her feelings. She would internalize all the things her mother did and said to her. So, she grew up having a hard time expressing how she feels. She felt she was not taken seriously.

Now, she has her guard up and trust issues. Personally speaking, she has been emotionally, physically, and mentally enslaved by rejection. Rejection had her feeling spiritually disconnected and neglected. It made her feel helpless, worthless, and selfless. It had her disengaged, in doubt, living in fear, experiencing emotional pain, sadness, and depression, thinking negatively, thinking about suicide, and living with low self-esteem. Myra started to believe she was living with cold-hearted parents. *Emotionally Rejected!*

Her parents always compared her to other people's kids. For example, they would say, "Oh, look at Sè (Sister) Marie's daughter, Belinda. She goes to church, is a nurse, and goes to nursing school. She has no boyfriend, drives a BMW car, and still lives with her parents. She cooks and cleans the house and respects her parents. Why can't you do that? Why can't you be like her? What are you doing with your life? You think you are going to sit around and do nothing with your life?" Meanwhile, you are trying to figure out what you want out of life because your parents have instilled in you to become either a doctor, a lawyer or a nurse when that's not even your interest. Or you can have a great man in your life but because he has dreads and works as the cable guy, he is considered a bum (street dude), looked down upon; he doesn't fit their "requirements." According to the Haitians, a good man must be God-fearing, a doctor, never married, have no children, smell good, dress in suits, be well-groomed, well-mannered, drive a nice car, be respectful, and willing to spend money on your mom. *Perfection!*

Imagine being in the car with your dad driving home and he is talking your ear off, just lecturing you about life. Next thing you know he starts pointing at random people, homeless people, drug-addicted people, saying this is going to be you "talking about give me five cents, please. Give me 5 cents, please." (I know he didn't mean any harm). In your mind, you are thinking I will not be like these homeless people or drug addicts or these random people begging for change. He's laughing and making jokes as if it's funny. Myra thought to herself, that is not funny. I am not about to start asking people to give me five cents, please. I guess that was his way of saying I want you to be better than that. Instead of feeding into it. It encouraged her to do and be better.

Parents know how to put such much pressure on you to make life very complicated. And because they have been doing this for so long, you live to prove them wrong, with every chance you get. Now you become defensive and feel as if you have to prove people wrong when they say or feel otherwise. You create unrealistic expectations for yourself, trying to be this perfect, innocent child to give your parents something to talk about. In the same instance, you never want to be seen as the bad child or doing wrong because your parents put you on a high pedestal or have high expectations for you that you have no room to mess up. God, forbid you do fall short. Don't let them know or find out. It will be the end of it. *Perfection proven!*

Her trust issues came from her having a hard time trusting herself and her mother. She did not believe in herself or trust herself in doing great things. Because her mother judged her and thought negatively of her ever since she was told she was being touched (abused). She would accuse her of doing things when she wasn't doing any wrong. That is why she became a rebellious child at a young age, in her preteen. She wanted her mother to be the person she can run to without being religious. She was honestly a child who just wanted a little freedom to explore and discover life. She felt her mother didn't have faith in her or trust her. As a mother, you should know your child better than a stranger. It was sad to know that, outside her home, the community or teachers knew her better than her parents. She would watch other parents speak well of their children and know their children better than the child knew themselves. Don't get me wrong. Myra loves her mother, no matter the circumstances, her mother has been there for her through it all. She grew closer to her aunts because she could be honest with them, and speak to them freely about her problems and feelings. They understood her without judgment and address her wrongdoing. This caused her to grow closer to her aunts on both sides of the family. Overall, she has learned a lot about her mother's character and who she is as a woman. Her mother is a very sweet woman. She has a huge heart and shares her love. She just wished her mother would have given her that space too. *Trust Denied.*

Now that Myra is an adult, she started expressing herself more freely, when she speaks, it comes off disrespectful because she was not fully healed or free for unforgiveness. All that resentment was built up inside. People who loved her did not deserve the disrespect or rude response. However, she was still operating from a place of hurt and not knowing how to let it go. When speaking to her parents, she would speak in a high voice as if she is ready to attack. She is in a place of learning to forgive herself, her mother, and those who she hurt as well as those who had hurt her, along the way. She didn't get validation from her parents. She felt she didn't feel trusted, loved, or cared for. She lived her entire life proving her parents wrong, trying to defend herself with every chance she got. It became overwhelming to show them that she is smart, wise, has a beautiful soul, and a child who was not as rebellious as other children. She had enough to prove to them that she was not a failure. She had more to life and whatever she desires and wants out of life, she shall have it. As she becomes older, she has had enough of living for them. Now it is time to live for herself and move forward. Myra had to exhale the old to inhale new air. She needed to leave the past behind and live in the present and make a better space for her mental state. It's challenging to forgive, but as time goes by, she tries her best to allow love to overcome the hurt she's been enduring. She decided to seek counseling from someone who is well-established and is passionate about her craft, someone who can guide her mentally and spiritually. I need to revisit that place of hurt.

Myra had learned that, even though she has been through negative times, her circumstances created the woman she is today. Myra believes that she can stand and not take bullshit from people and not care how people feel. In life, you need tough skin. I'm not that tough, but tough enough to stand. I can be heartless, which I'm not bragging about because I have hurt people along the way. Growing up, my parents dismissed my feelings as a child. They encouraged the notion that expressing how I felt was a sin or a crime. As if I was not supposed to have feelings and express them but suppress them. This is the reason why I grew up with tough skin, outwardly showing no compassion or cares, but inwardly crying. I started to feel like I was drowning. In the eyes of my mother, my tears were frowned upon, and my emotions were downplayed. So, I grew up with that same attitude that they showed me—not to care about people's feelings because they were staged, to laugh at their emotions when they were being expressive. Now, I'm disconnected because my dad never showed his emotions. After all, he internalized them. He never said I love you, so she doesn't know what it is.

When I hear I love you from someone who meant it, I was trying to sense and feel the same thing. Even when people say define love, it's hard for me to define it or know what love looks like or process it. Now, do you get it? So, when I smile or laugh, it's not because I want to express it. It became natural to be a second safe place which is hard to explain. It was a way of learning how to process what I have heard because I do not know how to process it. The hard part for me was trying to express how I feel, especially in relationships and I know communication is the most important key. Not being able to express yourself kills the moment, the relationship, and it becomes toxic to you and your partner. With the help of counseling, I was able to learn how to express myself by taking small steps. First, I was able to put the right words with the right faces. Then I did an exercise saying, "I feel this way because_____" and finishing the sentence. Yes, my parents created that dark side of me. For many years, I was not able to understand why I was like this, or why I was using negative thinking as a crutch and defensive mechanism and later shutting down, unable to express how I felt or continuing to internalize my feelings until I have no more room for anything. That's what causes you to have developmental diseases, illnesses, and sicknesses, which are curable with time and proper care. It took God to place me in a certain area in my life for me to realize a lot of things on my own even when I was aware of it. Not enough to say, there need to be a change in my life because the stressors- the depression were affecting me personally, socially, emotionally, physically, and mentally.

We have to realize our parents, too, probably were faced with the same experiences, or experienced life challenges differently from us through their parents, friends, relatives, teachers, boyfriends, girlfriends, or spouses. Our parent's experiences shaped and molded their character. No one was there to address their depression, unhappiness, or their demons within so as to help them not internalize it because they were taught many years ago to sweep it under the rug or not to say anything about it so the family won't look bad. What they didn't know is whatever they swept under the rug was becoming their identity and character, as well as affecting them internally, which is why they react the way they did. It hurts to know and is hard to understand why. Just know someone out there had it worse than you or has it worse than you.

We are all responsible for each other. How? By being that ear to listen and then show compassion. Imagine right now a child is being molested, raped, tortured, physically or sexually abused, or assaulted, and growing up having the same attitude or character you had. It could be worse or better. It takes an individual with a loving heart to revamp their way of thinking to help them heal from traumatic experiences and to remold themselves to see the greatest within themselves even with what they have experienced, and to let them know not to be a product of what they have experienced. Let's be each other's counselors and respect each other's confidentiality. That's how you gain loyalty and trust. We all have been hurt in some shape or form. Internalizing it won't help the situation to disappear; rather it will stagnant. It takes proper care and love to heal. Purge and purge. That's why forgiveness is important.

At times, we fear being rejected because we don't know how to handle rejection. It kills your self-esteem when someone or something is rejecting you. You start to feel lifeless or unworthy because you either gave your all or feared the unknown. The rejection came from somewhere. We all have experienced rejections, whether in a relationship, social environment, in our personal life, with ourselves or in a work environment. Rejection has been played out and the outcome of it is either positive or negative actions. Some people don't do well with rejections, so they start to stalk people to validate their feelings. For me, a part of me just wants to give up. I feel so alone at times. I want someone to talk to, but I don't have that person because people are seeing the negative side of things and can't help me solve the bigger picture. I hate being silent because I feel like I'm burying thoughts and expressions. I feel like my words are choking my soul. Sometimes when I come to someone, I think I can confide in for a piece of advice and that person turns around and makes me look like a fool, then I start to think why I trusted that person with my feelings in the first place. The purpose of my calling was to have someone to hear what is bothering me and to see the bigger picture. But you're so focused on the negative or keywords that you missed out on the root of the problem.

The person you trust and confide in should be the one to support and acknowledge what you are feeling. The reason the individual came to you in the first place is that they trusted you with information and trusted that you'll be able to guide them through. Maybe if you could impartially assess or evaluate the situation, there might be a better outcome. Oftentimes, people can be in such a confused state of mind that, even when the answer is right in front of their faces, they can still be blindsided by it. Or maybe the answer to the problem is not what they wanted it to be. Maybe you can help the individual strategize and look at the root of the problem in a better light or lens. My suggestion to you is to take off your lens of beliefs and put on a worldview lens to see what the individual is voicing because no one wants to die feeling what's been bottled up inside of them for years that's been causing cancer, bitterness, and all types of diseases. Lend of the ear. Stop being so judgmental or so negative when someone comes to you for a piece of advice. Now there's a difference between being real and judging the situation. When an individual comes to you for advice, put yourself in their shoes. The individual's feelings may be so bottled up that they don't want to hear a different view of your opinion or what they should and shouldn't do if there is anything. Help the individual to see the big picture of why or restate what it sounds like for this individual because then it makes you and the person feels that not only are you hearing them, but you're also understanding and acknowledging how the individual feels and how the individual sees things. Once you're able to do that, then you can make recommendations using a clear lens not using your belief system. Sometimes what you believe in and what the individual believes in are two different things and you should not impose your values upon the individual based on what decision you would make.

We all have our journey. I own my path, I own my stories, I own my downfalls and I own my mistakes. Your judgment should be a nonfactor when someone comes to you seeking advice or an ear just to spill out what they feel. I was living in denial, making myself believe that I forgave you for what you did to me when I never did. I wanted wholeheartedly, but I couldn't, I didn't, because I kept opening up new chapters in my life that I had no business opening up. But when an individual can sincerely heal and close that chapter, and not live in denial and be honest with themselves about how they are feeling and acknowledge it and take it for what it is, and never look back at it again. Release unforgiveness and say to yourself, "I am now healed. I can now move on and move forward." When you harbor unforgiveness, it makes room for bitterness, and you start to look at everything around you in a negative light. Yeah, your energy becomes negative, your surroundings become negative, and your thinking becomes negative even when you try to have positive thoughts. The negative overshines the positive. It's like having a dark cloud following you for the rest of your life. For the positive shine to come, you must release the root of the problem—your traumatic experiences and the voices. Be transparent with yourself. Sometimes you may not get the validation you may seek and maybe you'll never get closure, but you must be able to accept it and move forward. Sometimes you do get closure and it causes you to become a better person. The person you were is not the person you're going to be, is not the person you going to project, because you can make a change.

For example, rapper Nipsey Hussle came from the streets, but he decided one day to make a change. He started by giving back to his community. He started by buying the whole neighborhood. He created a new platform. He came from a negative and turned it into a positive. He didn't get closure, but who knows if he did or not. The point is he turned a negative situation into something great. That's how he was able to have a legacy and his name will forever be a legacy. Now his street bears his name and when you look at the name, you'll remember the history behind it. The schools he created, the store he invested in, the neighborhood he invested in. I'm pretty sure somebody's going to carry that baton. Even if the baton was to fall tomorrow, someone else will pick it up and continue the race. It will continue because not only did Nipsey create a legacy, but he also created a name.

That's how you want your character to be. You want to be able to finish what you started in a positive light. Forget about the negative. That happened to you, but it's shaping you for a better position. Anyone with a high position or title or elevated to another level went through something, that prepared them for where they are now. Also, do not judge an individual in their brooding place, their place of trials because you do not know where God is about to take them or place them. When God releases them, handle them well. You never know what a person went through or how hard they fought or anything to be where they are right now. Life is a f***** up place, a f***** up journey, but guess what? Greatness comes out of it if you'll allow it to. If you take the negative and turn it into a positive, I'm pretty sure it'll all come together for good. Look at our lives—how much negativity we have put in our lives and how we can turn it into a positive.

Society says these are excuses because you can overcome these things which is true. But the part society forgot it takes time to reconstruct the mindset and the things you were exposed to. It takes a certain journey, path, and experience to adapt to new things. It takes a certain individual or individuals to shape and mold positive thinking and to show and express love and gratitude. These things don't happen overnight. As a child, we were exposed to new things every day that shaped and molded our character. Every day we are revamping, whether we see it or believe it. It's happening. We pick up on someone else's identity. Go and spend four hours with an individual and see how fast you pick up on a word they may say or something they do. You will start to do it unconsciously. The point is, we become our parents' bad habits. We create our character based on what we were taught or what we perceived to be true. It either made us or broke us. If my parents didn't have that attitude, maybe my life would have been shaped differently. The outcome is you can always turn a negative into a positive. I can learn how to love creating what I want love to look like—it's just playing with imagination. It sounds cheesy, but the reality is manifesting what you want. In the Bible, John 1:1 (KJV) says, "In the beginning, was the Word, and the Word was with God, and the Word was God." Our thoughts create words, our words manifest into reality with time. I can attract those things by surrounding myself with them and allowing myself to have love in my life. I start first with myself. It will be a challenge, but I will master it.

Beyonce Knowles said in her song "Me, Myself, and I, she states 'I have me, myself, and I is all I got in the end, that is what I found out. And ain't no need to cry. I took a vow that from now on. I'm going to be my own best friend.'" What if in that me, myself, and I is where I discover my worst inner me… In that lonely place where I have to face those demons, those struggles, the real me, the things I did not want to face. Here I am facing them to become a better me. If I have to better myself in those moments, I will. At the end of the day, when it is all set and done you are stuck with and have only me, myself, and I. Just make sure in me, myself, and I, you don't live there so you do not get stuck in your thoughts.

PERCEPTION: ME, MYSELF, AND THEM

I have learned throughout my journey that I can be my own worst enemy. Or people can bring the enemy out of me. I used to think everyone was against me. I would self-sabotage myself. I was not happy with my body image, my self-image, comparing myself to other women on social media. I was always in defensive mode and it has stemmed from being compared to other children as a child, having to pay the price for my siblings actions, being blamed for everything, and being bullied. As the first generation, the oldest of four was challenging, coming from a strict religious Haitian Christian home. It came with a lot of responsibilities. I had to live up to so many expectations and set the bar (be a great example) for my siblings. I can surely tell you, if I messed up, I will be the reason my siblings did too. At some point, I practically raised my siblings. I had to represent the family as well as extended family at a high standard due to reputation, respect, perception purposes and status. If I didn't, it would be a disappointment to them. Along the way, it created a struggle for me and formed different identities and new perceptions of me. I remember battling between me, myself and I, it was challenging trying to be me vs who my parents wanted me to be. I was trying to live up to a perfect life to accommodate my happiness and theirs. When I became pregnant with my oldest son. It changed my parents' perception of me I felt they no longer viewed me as "the perfect daughter" but the daughter who will struggle working for the rest of her life with no future, due to having a baby out of a wedlock. I had to move out of my parent house and move into my own apartment, due to my dad protecting his image and reputation as a pastor. As well as living by the biblical principles and laws. More so, I was upset, angry, alone, confused, and betrayed. I felt ashamed, disown, and became extremely depressed. My whole childhood, I was taught to be conservative and resilient and walk a very Christian fine line. I hated myself for slipping up and not living up to their expectations. I lived in regret and blame for letting myself down, failing my family, and those who looked up to me. All in all, it motivated and pushed me to prove them wrong.

Haitian parents are known to be strict, overprotective, defensive, take everything to the next level, love to blame, make assumptions, and super religious. Fortunately, my parents were always tough on us which is the reason I am tough on myself. No matter what I do, it has to be perfect. I mean, **EVERYTHING**. Well, my relationship with my parents as a child was lukewarm. Don't get me wrong. I love my parents with all my heart. I did not see eye to eye with them. I held onto resentment, and they became a trigger to me. My parents are loving people, but my mom can be judgmental and draw negative assumptions, and don't let her get upset. I would have a conversation with her and the first thing that comes out of her mouth would be judgment and negativities. She would complain about everything I do and wear and force me into her style of dressing. As I reflect, I remember my mother sharing on how she work very hard to buy my siblings and I expensive clothing and shoes, teach us the importance of wearing a watch and perfume, to look presentable and be well respected. She even taught us the way we dressed will have people show us respect and some class.

When it came to choosing our future husband or dating. She always mentioned to her daughters, as a metaphor, if a man can't buy you panties, avoid being in a relationship with them, because he won't take care of you. My mom wouldn't let me date or be in a relationship until I was finished with college and settled in my career. Growing up in a Haitian Christian household, Christianity was the foundation of the family, then school, and home. You could not have any kinds of friends, date anyone, settle for less, have a certain career (only doctor, lawyer, engineer, teacher, and RN nurse), dress a certain way, and blah blah blah. I began to shut my culture off because of expectations. They were too much to live up too. The responses I would receive made me look at my own reflection differently. Because of this, I grew up being Americanize, thinking negatively about myself, hating who I was, and not loving me. I became depressed, sadden, and going through identity crises.

And my dad? We had a good relationship. He was more easy-going than my mom and relaxed, but loved "the God" (Laughing out loud). He was a talker; he can talk your ear off. For those who knew my dad, he loves talking about God and preaching the Bible. At times, you do not want to hear it, especially if your whole life was about church. He was about his work and church. I had my ways with my dad. He understood me and was lenient when it comes to being more independent. My mom was the one who wanted me to be co-dependent because she felt I was not old enough to be taught independence. Truth be told, my dad also had his negative ways that I did not agree with such as always comparing me to someone in the streets or stating I would grow up to be a beggar if I didn't have a job, finish school or have a good head on my shoulder. Now looking back, he wanted the best for his children. Honestly, it shaped me to wanting to prove something or them wrong.

Because of the dead weight I have carried over the years. I became my own critic and overly analyzed people's word and actions, create my own assumptions, and doubted myself. All it did was lead me to the road of self-destruction, self-affliction, and me against the world. When you start to think everyone is against you, it's really you against yourself and everyone else. You don't know who to trust or believe because you think everyone is your enemy. My confession is that I would allow the voices in my head, the talks I have with self, hold me back, making me think no one was for me, would support me, love me, cared about me, make me out to be a fool, or was not good enough, attractive enough, or worth it. I was causing my own affliction and was triggered by:

1. Past hurt and past pain.

2. Failing to see me for me (God revealing who I truly am- accepting my flaws).

3. Negative thoughts- the battle of the mind.

4. My Pride – proving I do not need you. I can do it all by myself. I can do it without you (getting in God's way).

5. Failing to heal; created mental bondage and recycling pain.

6. My feelings and emotions

The real deal is that when your past haunts you, it makes you go crazy, like losing your mind. You want to move forward, but you have a dark cloud surrounding you and you have nothing better to offer but negativity or views. You become stuck. I was in a dark place of my life, where everything about me was negative. When I wanted to speak or seek the positive, I saw the negative too. I attracted the negative for so long that it became my lifestyle. It was destroying my self-esteem, and my relationship with people because I was operating in my emotions, hurt, and pain. When you experience real hurt, your world starts crashing down (this did not stem from my past relationship. We are talking about overall hurt and pain). If you are not mentally stable or strong, it will turn into bitterness and you into a cold-hearted person. That was me—cold-hearted and unhappy, but that wasn't my intention. I knew what I wanted but just didn't know how to attract it. When I received real love, I threw it away. I couldn't tell between the fake and the real. It was hard to differentiate. I would put my heart on the table and give my all and my heart and feelings were taken for granted to the point I became hard-shelled, defensive, and guarded so people wouldn't hurt me. Before you hurt me, I would hurt you first. Because being hurt is painful. For some, it's like rolling all over your grave, and for others, the pain is mastered. In a sense, I mourned so now I can move forward.

I was like that until I fell in love. I gave my love out freely and nothing was returned, but burnt bridges, false assumptions, misunderstandings, karma, lies, cheating, abuse, and misuse. I will never forget being in a relationship where I got used to this man's patterns of cheating and lies. Although he said he changed, I kept seeing those patterns of behaviors and I eventually became immune to them such that I couldn't tell between the fake and the real. In my mind, those same behaviors he displayed with me were probably the same behaviors he shared with other women. It drove me crazy, dealing with sleepless nights, reckless nights of tears, wishing, hoping, and praying that I can be removed from the situation. But I would still go back to the place and the person that broke me because I didn't know any better. I was in love with the pain I was causing myself and I became immune to the pain.

Happiness was what I wanted but could never get. Why? Because my subconscious was producing and attracting negative thoughts. I tried to fight those thoughts, but I could not seem to shake them off. Thoughts are very powerful, whether you believe them or not. What you think you become. What comes out of the mouth is what is in the heart. At night, I would question God and ask how he can promise me something and I am living the opposite of what he promised nor am I seeing any results. I started to feel that prophets were false prophets and did not believe in the promises. My faith would grow weary and, if you are not careful or strong, you will fall. My spirit man was saying otherwise. I went on Facebook and this prophetess had a post about Ephesians 4:32 (WEB): *"And be kind to one another, tender hearted, forgiving each other, just as God also in Christ forgave you."* Then I've decided to read Ephesians 4:17-31 (WEB):

"This I say therefore, and testify in the Lord, that you no longer walk as the rest of the Gentiles also walk, in the futility of their mind, 18 being darkened in their understanding, alienated from the life of God because of the ignorance that is in them, because of the hardening of their hearts. 19 They, having become callous, gave themselves up to lust, to work all uncleanness with greediness. 20 But you didn't learn Christ that way, 21 if indeed you heard him, and were taught in him, even as truth is in Jesus: 22 that you put away, as concerning your former way of life, the old man that grows corrupt after the lusts of deceit, 23 and that you be renewed in the spirit of your mind, 24 and put on the new man, who in the likeness of God has been created in righteousness and holiness of truth.

25 Therefore putting away falsehood, speak truth each one with his neighbor. For we are members of one another. 26 "Be angry, and don't sin." Psalm Don't let the sun go down on your wrath, 27 and don't give place to the devil. 28 Let him *who stole steal no more; but rather let him labor, producing with his hands something that is good, that he may have something to give to him who has need. ^{29} Let no corrupt speech proceed out of your mouth, but only what is good for building others up as the need may be, that it may give grace to those who hear. ^{30} Don't grieve the Holy Spirit of God, in whom you were sealed for the day of redemption. ^{31} Let all bitterness, wrath, anger, outcry, and slander be put away from you, with all malice."*

The chapter was speaking to me and about me because of the heart I had. I knew I had to renew my mind. I wanted to so I kept praying and reading from time to time. I wanted to seek God first in my journey and accept all challenges without being weak-minded or weak in my emotions. That's where I was always in my feelings. I wanted to master my emotions by self-regulating them. I knew for sure; that I would overcome and master them. I would enter the next month in a better state of mind, manifest positivity, and not be or feel defeated. I seemed to keep hurting myself by revisiting my past hurt due to triggers that left an open wound or kept a hole in my heart. I needed to be delivered from struggling with my past, overthinking, internalizing my thoughts, feelings, everything that occurred in my life, and hurting me. Trying to overcome it and have peace within was a challenge because I had to learn to let go. I felt like I was in the dark because I was always angry. My mind was cluttered, cloudy, and not free. I tried to remove that dark cloud. I prayed and listened to gospel music and vowed to be free from the dark cloud and prayed for God to remove that dark cloud and He did.

I can now think much better than before. My spirit is renewed and fresh. I love like never and my heart is right and pure. What used to bother me, don't. My spirit is free. I have a demeanor that makes people want to know who I am. I am now more confident than ever before. I am everything I ever imagined myself to be. I can now be still and listen to the voice of God and prosper in His grace. Once I started to seek God, everything around me changed. My business started growing and increasing and everything my heart desired; came to pass. I am free—free from hurt, free from pain, free from bondage, free from my self-infliction. Lastly, let's learn to embrace our true self/ identity as an independent individual separate from our family. If I can do that, you can too.

IDENTITY STOLEN

"You start to find your identity in who you are around. You start to find your value in who you are around. Who I am around is who I am.? You start to get caught up, but they will all fail you, even your good friends. Look at Jesus, Peter denied him, and his friends fall asleep on him. Don't build your life on your fans, followers, and friends. They cannot give you what you truly need. Don't put all of yourself into your friends because when they leave you, you will lose you. Your friends can't tell you who you are. They didn't create you."

-Charles Metcalf (YouTube, 2019)

Have you ever heard your parents say, "I don't like those types of friends" or someone else say, "They don't look like the type of friends you should hang around?" It is because they don't match your style or your identity, or they are not a good reflection of who you are or stand for. At times, we think the friends we have best represent us, or we represent them due to the same interest or because we share aspirations or long history. The friends we made, in the beginning, may have had great intentions and some may not. As we start to get older, our values change, our career path changes, our life changes, and our goals change, but not our friends. What we wanted then is not what we want now. We either add more friends to the circle or keep the ones we always had. We start to do things we never did before or were exposed to, whether good or bad. As we get older, the more we surround ourselves with these people, we start to pick up habits, language, or behavior they have. Personalities, words, and traits do rub off naturally. Think about it? Who you surround yourself with, you become. What you think of yourself, you are. Who you speak to, reflects you. Choose your company wisely. Audit your friends and make sure you are in the right surroundings.

Your identity was formed by those you surrounded yourself with, your thoughts and behavior were influenced by those who planted negative seeds, and your character was based on people's lifestyles. There's a saying: "You need to know where you sit inside the larger network of the social community." Who do you identify yourself with? Since childhood, you probably created an identity that was not your own and have been surrounding yourself with lost souls. You were probably sitting and eating with soul drinkers, and backbiting savages. Then adapted to their identity of the savages and dressed it up with loyalty, but deep down inside, loyalty wasn't present. Although they were presenting who they were, you ignored the red flags. Your investment in the friendship became devalued because no exchange was being returned—our relationship wasn't adding any value; it was subtracting.

Ever wonder, I was losing everything I invested in even my own identity. My friends stole my identity, stripped it down, reinvented it, and created their own. My name was no longer my name; I became a staged play. I became one of them and didn't even know when I converted. My own identity was robbed due to fear and insecurities and my wanting to be accepted due to low self-esteem. It became too late to save the image I held dear because my name was dragged onto the display. After years of being shaped and molded, I realized my circle wasn't my circle. My circle was not my cure. I became more infested. My heart became colder and dark.

Instead of a tight bond, we created a circle within a circle and categorized each other. Bridges were being crossed; friendship was being burnt; our loyalty for each other had died. The respect was no longer there. Our friendship become a mental disorder because we all are diagnosed with PTSD. Now, we were looking into other friendships for treatment plans and interventions, looking to be accepted by others for a better understanding and solutions to cure our problems. Loyalty doesn't exist if you're burning bridges and crossing them while holding up a sign that says yield, don't cross. I guess that's life, just *not* mine. When you know your identity, you don't have to feel like you have many strings attached to many people because you know who you are. When you know who you are, you won't have to find where you fit. You will know how valuable you are. You do not have to live as someone else to prove a point. Be you naturally and beautifully.

YIELD LADIES

Quotes you often hear:

"Birds of a feather, flock together."
"Be around eagles and soar."
"You are who you spent the majority of your time with."
"Show me your friends, I'll show you your future."
"They are your identity."
"Loyalty is about people who stay true to you behind your back"
"Loyalty is consistency"
"If they stand by you during the bad times, they deserve to be there during the good times"

Ever had a girlfriend or girlfriends you grew up with, who knew about your past, but didn't know about your future or what great purpose God has for your life? Ever had a girlfriend or girlfriends that mean well, but loved drama, talked about everyone else's drama, and made jokes except joking about their life drama which they minimize? Ever had a girlfriend or girlfriends who turned your family or sibling against you? Ever had a girlfriend or girlfriends who thought they were just perfect, that they couldn't do any wrong? Ever had a girlfriend or girlfriends who thought they knew so much about you, but knew so little? Ever had a girlfriend or girlfriends who supported you and were always there for you, but thought it was alright for them to talk bad about you? They pretended to be by your side but turn you, compete because they didn't want you to succeed. They are jealous and envious to see greatness within you.

Quick Gem: Sometimes, it may not be your friends, it could be people with titles, higher positions, or individuals that are older than you, that want to silence you because they can see your future or want to be you. Or had the opportunity that you had and mishandle their position or fear you will take their position, title, fans, audience, clientele, etc. Because of this, they come against you, spread rumors about you, turn people against you, and speak ill of you. If you are not careful, they can consume you and form you to be just like them and you missed out on someone great because of their demise.

They knew you had the potential to be great, but, because they feared your success or your greatness, they started to minimize you. They told you one thing, but behind your back, they were saying another. They talked about your failures or your struggles to make themselves look good and you, bad. God was hiding you so when you came out, they would feel guilty. What they did not know was that God has a way of showing up and showing out. He has a way of taking you from a deep place and placing you in greatness, around greatness, in better situations where people ask how you got there.

There are messed-up friendships out here. Some friends will use you up until they can't use you anymore. Some friends set you up just so they could say, "I thought we were on the same page." Some friends will show you their true colors. Friends that showed up to your event just to see if it would be a success. Friends who would call just to speculate on your life so they could go talk about it behind your back. They loved to see you fail. They loved to see you hook up with the wrong person just so they could talk badly about you. They loved to know that you are doing wrong because they hate the fact you are doing good. They loved to see that you're just like them so you could have something in common and they could talk about it, just so they could say you are not as good as they thought after all.

Those are the type of friends you don't want in your life. You don't want to entertain them because they will never level up mentally. Real friends don't set you up so they can get glorified or make you look like a failure. But know this: all the setups that they put on your life are going to return to them one way or another. You could tell what kind of heart a person has just by staring into their eyes. Looking into someone's eyes is like looking deep down in their soul. The reality is; that these frenemies will never understand the decisions you make or the path you've decided to take. "Hey, I don't expect them to be; the same way I don't understand their journey as well." The thing is we are not supposed to understand each other's path or journey. The point is to make sure that we get to our destiny or reach our goal, no matter what. Regardless, the love and support of each other are all we need.

Friends are supposed to love you even when you decide to go on your path to do better for your life. They are not supposed to understand your path; their job is to help, support, and motivate you while you're on this journey. Friends open doors for you while you walk through the doors and make sure the path you are creating is worth creating. They are not supposed to open the doors, stand there, watch you fail, mock or laugh at your success. They are not supposed to bash you and make you feel wrong for making life-changing decisions. They are not supposed to criticize you or make you feel uncomfortable for making sacrifices. They are not supposed to talk about your failures. Even when you fall, they should lift you and push you even closer to your walk of life. It's not a race or a competition of who is getting there first or last. They should not be trying or setting up a trap because they feel you are Missy Goodie Too Shoes.

Friends should not feel intimidated by you or each other's successes because you can always help each other create their successes or make room for a better portfolio. What kind of friend becomes jealous of another one's success? Or why would you not want your friend to be successful? At the end of the day, their success makes you look good. At times, you play a role in helping them become successful. You may not reach the same level of success as your friend does, but because your friend reflects you, you will reap the same seed your friend planted because your friend will instill that same success knowledge in you or expose you to the same environment your friend is now in.

Sometimes your friend's past may not be your past, but because you reflect on your friend, your friend's path can create a new path for you through your faithfulness, supportiveness, obedience, and humbleness. Ever heard the pastor say, "If God can do it for them, then He can do it for me" or "If God did it for them, I know that I'm next?" Another way of looking at this is from the movie *Girls Trip*. Towards the end, Ryan got Sasha a gig as her journalist. A true friend knows when one makes it, we all make it. We all can create greater success when we combine resumes to have great ammo because you are creating a larger network; their network becomes your network as well. It's about holding each other down, accountable, making sure the goals are met, and not letting anyone in the group slack off. If someone does, the group steers the person back on track. True friendship doesn't envy or create jealousy. True friendship celebrates, shows appreciation, and speaks life and words of wisdom to show a friend that the time and energy invested is not a waste. True friendship breaks bread together.

Yes, we all have our flaws and demons, but with those flaws, we should uplift each other and turn them into strengths. We should not dig deeper holes or add more fuel to the fire. Yes, with friendship, there will be a secretive journey one must take, but it doesn't change where the friendship stands. Loyalty is, at its best, what you do or say when your friend is not around and that's what counts, not what is being done in their presence. Reconsider your position as a friend. Have you made a positive impact on your friend's life, or have you absorbed all that you need to destroy your friend's life?

Loyalty: the quality of being loyal, a strong feeling of support or allegiance. Synonyms: faithfulness, bond, devotion, trueness, true-heartedness, dedication, commitment, reliability, constancy. Loyalty creates opportunity and makes room for growth. (dictonary.com)

Urban Dictionary: Making something or someone a priority and doing so in small and discrete but meaningful ways. **Staying true** to someone or something even when other things call attention. **A way of showing support for a person or thing.** (urbandictonary.com)

Friend: a person whom one knows and with whom one has a bond of mutual affection, typically exclusive of sexual or family relations. Synonyms: companion, boon companion, bosom friend, best friend, close friend, intimate, confidante, confidant, familiar, soul mate, alter ego, second self, shadow, playmate, playfellow, classmate, schoolmate, workmate, ally, comrade, associate; sister, brother; informal pal, bosom pal, buddy, bosom buddy, chum, spar, sidekick, cully, crony, main man; informal bezzie, mate, oppo, china, mucker, butty, bruvver, bruv; informal marrow, marra; informal amigo, compadre, paisan, homie, bro; informal homeboy, home girl; informal gabba; informal offsider; archaic compeer; rare fidus Achates (dictonary.com)

Friendship: the emotions or conduct of friends; the state of being friends. A relationship between friends. Synonyms: relationship, friendly relationship, close relationship, attachment, mutual attachment, alliance, association, close association, bond, tie, link, union; amity, camaraderie, friendliness, comradeship, companionship, fellowship, fellow feeling, closeness, affinity, rapport, understanding, harmony, unity; intimacy, mutual affection; cordial relations. Antonyms: enmity, a state of mutual trust and support between allied nations. (dictionary.com)

Sister: a woman or girl in relation to other daughters and sons of her parents. A close female friend or associate, especially a female fellow member of a labor union or other organization. Synonyms: female sibling; informal is; rhyming slang skin and blister, comrade, friend, partner, associate, colleague. (dictonary.com)

If I am loyal to you and I call you my sister, it means my loyalty is to you- my sister- translates to, what is mine is yours, my money is your money, my headache is your headache when I travel, you travel, you need it I have it, I need it you have it, my struggle is your struggle, either I guide you through it or help you through it. I struggle with the word loyalty myself because it was misused by peers who didn't even know what the word meant themselves, as well as my perception of what I thought or wanted loyalty to look like. Loyalty is hard to find because everyone is out for themselves or maybe, they don't know what loyalty really means or looks like. You do not use the word loyalty or say I am loyal.

Now, there are loyal people out here and it is a matter of surrounding yourself with the right people, at the right place, at the right time. When you think of the word loyalty, what comes to mind? Do they fit the criteria? The word itself stands alone. Loyalty is never burning bridges. Once the bridge is burned, there's no tracing back to where we left off. The evidence is no longer there. If you do burn a bridge, make sure it is worth burning. Know that it hurts when someone tries to compete with you about getting married, having a baby, having a house, being in a career, and setting goals to accomplish whether long-term or short term when life itself is a competition. That's enough to drive you up a wall. Why would anyone want to deal with that when the definition of friendship is to support each other to get to the next level?

We tend to forget the true meanings of words that we use so loosely. For example, we start a new job, build a great relationship with that specific co-worker based on the same interests or perceptions, and now consider her your friend, not knowing she has an agenda. You know her for two weeks and now she is sis, sista, bestie, best friend, friend, and loyal. I kind of blame grade school for having us address our classmates as friends even though they were teaching us how to respect one another and how to treat each other. Our teachers taught us to use the word "friends" too early, instead of teaching us ways to address them as peers or classmates. Charles Metcalf said it best in his sermon, *Too Many Friends/All Strings Attached*. This is a great sermon you must hear. I've found it on YouTube. The strings that we choose, the friends we saw and chose to do life with, are shaping your future. You agree with, look and act like the people you are with. The people you are walking with will have an impact on and shape your identity. He stated, "When you walk with the wise, you become wise. When you walk with a fool, you will become a fool. Everyone needs friends around them, however, everyone around you is not your friend. What we have are either fans, followers, or friends. **Fans** are different than friends. Fans like you for what you do, and what you produce. When you are a fan of someone, you think highly of them. They can encourage you, inspire you, compliment you, and make you feel good about yourself. They are only connected to you for what you do. We keep fans so close in our lives to please them because they are making us feel good. When someone does what you do, better than you do, they will leave you. They were never there for you. They will hurt you very badly when you allow them into your life because they were not there for you, they don't care about you. Many of us have fans, and we are trying to live our lives to impress people who don't even care about us. Don't cut them out, recognize their category. **Followers** are different than fans. A follower is closer, you may choose your followers. They will choose whether they want you to speak into their life. They will see something in you, or what they like about you, and they will decide to do life with you. Followers will help you reach your purpose in life. Followers won't always understand your true purpose or take a leap of faith with you when it doesn't make sense to them. They are like scaffolders. **Friends**, real friends, who care about you, know what is on the inside of you, and know who you are. Jesus had three friends. You need people who know who you are to be with you. Friends you allow to see who you are, without having to wear a mask. They see purpose on the inside of you and are willing to fight for you. They are intimate. A true friend fight alongside you. A true friend fights against you, which means, they tell you when you are wrong or prideful. A true friend fight for you. You need people who will fight for you when you don't have the energy to fight your fight. Friends who will stand in front of you when you can't, pray for you, and be there for you.

We need each one of them: fans, followers, and friends. We are all these categories in other's people lives and recognize the place they hold in our life." (Youtube.2019)

We no longer know the meaning of true friendship. When you think of true friendship, you define it as someone who is there for you through thick and thin. An individual who has your back no matter what, an individual you can consider family, or an individual who can and will uplift you when you fall or pray with you in times of trouble. A friend is someone you can depend on. When you struggle, they can give you a helping hand. They can and will call you out when you are wrong and challenge you even when you are right. True friendship builds off loyalty. When real situations are exposed, they don't scatter or whisper to others. Real situations will expose real friends. In the book, *The People Factor: How Building Great Relationships and Ending Bad Ones Unlocks Your God-Given Purpose,* by Van Moody, which is a recommended book to read, Mr. Moody (2014) defines good and bad relationships whether the relationship is with family members, workers, friends, or associates. He speaks about synergy and says synergy is "people, groups or things coming together to produce something greater than any of them could ever produce alone." He also stated

"Relationships that bring synergy to your life will not only be win-win for you but they will also be of exponential value to you. They will multiply your potential and your impact so your abilities, plans, natural gifts, girls, and everything about your life functions at its optimum." What I love about this book is that it defines a healthy relationship and what it produces. A healthy relationship is to be surrounded by like-minded individuals; iron sharpens iron kind of relationships. A healthy relationship or true friendship is "finding winning synergistic friends" (Moody, 2014). Van Moody states, "The only way to build win-win, synergistic relationships is to develop them with the right people. And he also gives steps to finding a synergistic friend- listed below (p.g36, Moody, 2014). And I quote from Van Moody:

"Steps to Finding Synergistic Friends: The Components to Loyalty/True Friendship

1. Winning synergistic friends encourage greater faithfulness

2. Winning synergistic friends are character-driven

3. Winning synergistic friends will defend you

4. Winning synergistic friends love God more than they love you

5. Winning synergistic friends urge you to sow. They will encourage you to sow time, energy, finances, and other resources into worthy people, places, and activities because they want to see you experience the exponential benefits that result from generous, heartfelt giving.

6. Winning synergistic friends are committed to your future, not your past

7. Winning synergistic friends help you live a life of gratitude

Therefore, everyone in a relationship needs to win. If one or both parties feel they are losing, they are headed for trouble. You cannot run on empty with the people with whom you are in a relationship; you must pour into your life as you pour into theirs. Relational health grows and thrives in an environment of mutual benefit. The next step beyond mutual benefit is synergy; which enables everyone involved in a relationship to do exponentially more than they could do or be on their own. Negative synergy is as damaging as positive synergy is helpful in your life. Make the effort to prepare for synergy and become a better person (p.g36)." Now that I have spoiled Chapter Two of the book, purchase the book; it is a great read.

We all are looking for lifetime sisters who cheer us the same way they cherish themselves and support us the same way you support them. We are looking for friendships that evolve into family, friendships that are never dull, friendships that respect each other's struggles, friendships that honor each other, and the undeniable, not-so-perfect but just the right type of friendship. We are looking for the friends that will call us on our wrongs and not talk about it behind our backs, the ones who don't mock or laugh at our downfalls, but laugh together with us when we make it to the top and say, "Remember when you did x, y, and z?" My great friend, sister, and marriage family therapist mentioned to me, "Friendships are like a tree. Some are like the branches that break off and sometimes grow back, some are like the leaves that fall during seasonal changes, and some are like the roots that grow stronger through all stormy weathers." We won't have a perfect friendship, but as long as the loyalty is there, that's what matters.

We all have flaws and or inner demons we battle with within ourselves. We all have different upbringings, values, and belief systems, and think and see things differently. The point of this is to have true loyalty in your circle, where the investment is not a total loss, where the relationship has value, and where annuity and equity are provided and made. Let's practice kindness. Not only practice being generous in giving the best in tangible or materialist things but having a kind heart or spirit of wanting to be best and give the best in character in relationships.

So, redefine and reevaluate your circle of friends and or choose better relationships with individuals.

Now ask yourself these questions and reevaluate yourself as a friend:

1. Have you been loyal or brought something positive to the friendship?
2. Can your friendship bring or sisters call on you for mental support, financial support, or spiritual support- meaning give wisdom and great counsel?
3. Do you create a safe space or environment for them?
4. Do you create memories, spend quality time, and have great quality conversation?
5. Do you accept where they are and for who they are (during their transition of life)?
6. Do you consistently inspire them to their highest potential?

7. Do you give them the space to evolve, emerge, and make mistake without judgement? Still love and value them the same way they value you or vice versa?

Sometimes, we blame others, but sometimes the fault comes from us as well. I had to yield myself many times. After all, I knew I wasn't pouring into my friendships as I should because I was holding onto and dealing with past hurts. The way I envision relationships to be, they weren't what I expected due to my expectations. I wanted high-maintenance friends with high class to do luxurious things with, I was not that myself. Sometimes, we asked for something we are not. The reality of it, not all high maintenance friends are high maintenance, for some they are like just those so-called friendships you see on television shows: Love in HipHop or Married to Medicine or The Real Housewives of Atlanta. DRAMA!!! JUST DRAMA. So, yes, yield, ladies. Check yourself twice, then your circle. Your inner circle of friends or sisters should have quality not quantity, unselfish within their measure, loyal, kind, gives insight, wisdom, knows how to have fun, sacrifice, walk in love, and off course, have your back but corrects you when you are wrong- whether received or not. It is done in/with love. So, cry, laugh, live but most important create precious moments.

I have a confession. I must abide by this too. What I write applies to me as well, but not off limits. There's always room for growth and I am not perfect. These are the things I have thought about, recognized, realized, somewhat practiced along the way, of how I could become a better friend and sister. Some of the qualities I did not bring to the table after a while or maybe I was overly criticizing myself which I do a lot. I always imagined myself being that quality friend and more.

GEMs: One thing I do want to touch on is divine relationships. In this case, I am referring to anyone you consider a friend, sister, or brother. Off course, there are many other potential factors and definitions, but here I am giving a few pointers. Divine relationships are to help embarked us into another dimension- moves the agenda forward, uplift us, bring the pieces to the puzzles, open doors during a strategic time of our lives. And encourage, motivate, inspire, and sometimes can be spiritually therapeutic – provide wisdom and good counsel. Divine relationships can be long or short terms or can establish itself into a close or personal relationship. I truly believe, when God connects you with divine friendship or purposeful individuals to help up level your visions, bring positive vibes into your life, impact your life, doesn't quit on you, loyal to you, trustworthy according to their measures (because our Father do wants us to trust him more than anything), and can make sacrifices (within to their measures). It is like iron sharpens iron. You recognize the fruit that the relationship brings healing, favor, empowerment, the missing ingredient, love, hope, peace, laughter, restoration, provision, acceptance, and many more. Recognizing potential or great relationships is when you can see an amount of growth in your life, being able to find your own voice, and you guys benefit from each other.

Everyone is not perfect, but when we walk in love, give grace, and show mercy as well as forgiveness. You see the purity of the individual. Keep in mind we all have **FLAWS**. Divine relationships do not bring turmoil, negativity, jealousy into or in your life, nor ignore your wellbeing. Remember, what is divine does not divide, distract, or detract. Friendships, sistership, brothership or relationships of any kind should help activate, not only the plans and purpose God has for your life but what's within you. Find your true authentic self and being receptive of it. They should add and help multiple to your life and accelerate you. They may not be an expertise in the field; however, their heart speaks. The power a relationship brings should help expedite and expand ideas, visions, and plans. Your spirit should resonate with theirs. Some relationships will be a lifetime, and some may not. And that is fine.

At the end of the day, when the dynamic of the relationship changes or season has shifted. You should feel assured and confident enough that it paid off for the better. Regardless of anything, it was good while it lasted. You have some great highlights from that relationship, you can take away or learn from to grow or become that phenomenal, dope, powerful individual.

TRAUMA, WHO I AM?

TD Jakes said in his sermon, "Silence is like darkness. When the enemy tries to attack you, the first thing he does is shut your mouth. A noise disrupts your silence."

T.D. Jakes writes that in order to heal from trauma, "You need a burning desire for the future, the kind of desire that overcomes past fear and inhibitions. You will remain chained to your past and all the secrets therein until you decide: Enough is enough!"

https://www.tdjakes.com/posts/heal-your-heart-by-tapping-into-your-strength

Wondering how silence kills? Imagine being robbed of your childhood multiple times and having to remain silent. Imagine your predator, preying on your vulnerability as an innocent child, just to gain control and power. Imagine your parents telling you to shut up and not to say a word or debunking the fact that he touched you, and to stop lying. Just imagine being told, "Baby, don't tell nobody. Let's forget it even happened." Just imagine, being touched at the age of seven by multiple people and you haven't even hit puberty yet; you are just innocent and pure. Do you remember how it all started? It started with parents confiding in individuals with their child thinking those they **trust** or **least doubt** would harm their child or children.

How did silence kill? Silence killed me when I was touched by a close friend of the family extended relative and close family member. I was just a little girl, pure and innocent, and hasn't reached puberty yet. I did not understand what was happening or know anything about being sexually touched. I just knew the feeling was wrong. It happened right before my eyes. We were all sitting in the hallway of the apartment, with their mom, watching television. It was dark when he sat me down on his lap and rub his lower pelvic area against mine and started to rub on my flat chest. After he was done, he got up and went to the bathroom to clean off. Before he left, he gave me candy to silence me about what just happened. Imagine you going to a friend's house just to play, or your parents left you at a close neighbor's house to watch you while they go to work or run some errands. In another incident, I remember sitting near the kitchen watching my mom's friend cook. I do not remember how old I was. I believe I was probably seven or eight years old.

As my mom's friend was cooking, I heard her brother, who at the time was in high school, whispering come here, with his finger on his lips telling me to sheesh. Not thinking anything of it, I got up and started walking his way. He closed the room door and told me to stay quiet. He turned me around and started to unbutton my pants. I can hear him breathing heavily and was still a little clueless about what was to happen. Silent to the situation. As he was about to pull my pants down, his uncle walked in and startled him. His uncle was shocked to see what he had walked into and asked me to leave. As I was leaving the room, I overheard the uncle asking him if he was sick or whether he wants to go to jail? I heard the uncle say, "She is a child. What were you trying to do with her?" I went back to my chair and did not say a word. His sister, who was watching me, didn't even notice I left, from where I was sitting. When my mom came back, I couldn't tell her what had happened to me. I was afraid of what she would do or whether she would believe anything I had to say. I let that moment die within me. I buried the thought of it ever happening to me.

Plus, it is culturally taboo to discuss or expose, sexual or physical abuse and or domestic violence. Because it is a sensitive topic, we are told to brush it under the rug, not to discuss it, tell it, and for some, they doubt it or don't believe it. I've always thought you were safe in the arms of relatives. I really thought relatives could do you no harm because they are family and to be trusted. In this case, I wasn't. A weekend at an extended family house, turned out to be a traumatizing one. I do not remember how old I was. All I recall vividly was sharing a bed with a relative. While sleeping, this relative woke me up to participate in a sexual act. This relative had me touch a particular body part of theirs while this relative was touching mine. This relative was directing me on what to do for their pleasure. All I felt was wetness. While in the act, I became traumatized. Due to this, it created a discomfort for me and afraid to explore my body for healthy purposes. I started to have full of self-hatred, became shy, and insecure which is the reason I have difficulty with reconnecting with my sexual being. Because I was a child, I was scared to speak up about what had occurred, fearing no one would believe me, doubt me, or this individual would deny it or maybe cause a scene. I buried that situation and lived life as if this never happened to me. Until one day, my past traumas revisit me and I had recurring flashbacks of me being touched by those individuals. This brought awareness and the effects to why I have had sexual problems, relationship, and intimacy issues as well as my journey of discovering my womanhood.

From then on, I became silent—silent to the memories and buried every emotion and thought. Suicide was on my mind. At eleven years old, I wanted to end it all and questioned why I was going through this. Why was I be robbed of my womanhood? I could not even look at myself in the mirror and love myself because of shame and guilt. I felt dirty, ashamed, and worthless, so, why not kill me? My first suicide attempt was in front of my siblings and a neighbor who we considered a cousin. At that time, I hated my life and everything that had happened to me. There was too much going on. I was being bullied, feeling unpretty, disliking my self-image, hating the color of my skin and I felt my parents didn't love me. In the little knowledge of my ignorant mind, I assumed my mother disliked me and spoke lies about me due to false accusations after being touched but I was only a *kid*. I just wanted to die. I remember their faces, traumatized at a young age, watching me put a knife to my stomach while contemplating if I should take my life or not, or maybe hurt myself enough to be admitted to the hospital just to make my parents feel sorry and hurt.

At times, I wished I was adopted by my aunts because they treated me better. They understood me like the strangers in the streets. The strangers knew me better than my parents. All my parents knew was church and work. They didn't take the time to get to know their kids or spend time with their kids. I wanted to make them feel the pain I was feeling so they would give me the attention I needed. I thought of watching them scream, "No, please don't do it!" with tears rolling down their faces made me think twice but still trying to explain to them why I did not want to live. All I can remember was my little cousin putting her hands on her head crying and my little sister and brother saying why and no. I wanted to attempt it, but I didn't have the courage to do it. I put the knife away, ended up dialing 9-1-1 then I quickly hung up the phone. I didn't expect the phone call to be returned. But the operator called back asking, "What's your emergency?" and my father said, "There's no emergency. No one called and my mother gave me the "I'm going to beat the mess out of whoever called 9-1-1" look. I was able to get away with it because my mother's best friend from

Canada was visiting. She saved me from getting that Caribbean beating.

I was just tired of being misunderstood, my feelings being laughed at, never acknowledged, and always being accused of things I did not do. I was a little girl who was innocent, loving, motivated, determined, caring, spoiled, and all, but with a big heart. It used to bother me so much how strangers knew me better than my parents. Living under the roof of strict, religious, and overly protective parents created a rebellious child, rebellious enough to go against my parents' rules for my own happiness as a youth. In all honesty, all I wanted was to be loved, to be heard, and to be trusted with some freedom. The I love you only came after a butt whooping with a long lecture to why they did what they did. I'll never forget being mock as a child for being emotional. I was laughed at me and called ugly for crying. In my head, I thought, "That's evil. Why would you mock me for crying?" I couldn't express how I felt without hearing judgmental remarks or statements.

During my second attempt of suicide, I locked myself in the bathroom crying, contemplating. I believed. I was a pre-teen at that time, dealing with low self-esteem, reoccurring memories of being sexually touched, being bullied, disliking my mom, feeling unloved, felt restraint. So much was going on. I hated my life. I couldn't have a normal childhood like any other child. Imagine growing up in a Haitian household, for most children, not being able to go outside to play with other children, having to stay in the house all day, can't participate in after school activities, trips, or programs, no friends, no birthday parties or attending any form of celebrations, because you are Christian, no sleepovers or spending the night out only by trusted family members, having a curfew to be home after school or being monitored everywhere you go, being whopped with a belt called *baton* or *ajenou* called kneeling for hours on a grater or having one leg up and one leg down due to negative behaviors. If one foot touched the floor, you would get a beaten. I recalled these forms of punishment for not bringing home A's or B's, talking back, a phone call from school, allowing my sibling to misbehave or just being a disobedient child, rude, disrespectful, or negative behaviors that is considered unacceptable to them.

As I grew older, all my childhood traumas affected my self-esteem, my self-image, my character, who I was developing to be, and my sexuality. I became afraid—afraid of me, afraid of relationships, afraid of my own body, even the great men around me. I became suppressed, oppress, and depressed because I became my worst inner-me (enemy). I started creating negative thoughts about myself and thinking negatively about everything. I couldn't look at myself the same. When someone would complement me, I would say thank you, but question it. If a guy was interested in me, I would think he only wanted me for what was in between my legs. Or he didn't really think I'm beautiful. I would look at myself in the mirror and find everything that was wrong with me. I didn't like the structure of my face, my body weight or type, my skin complexion, the way I talked, or my voice; I just hated myself. The only things I appreciated and loved were my plum oranges—my breasts. The only attractive things were my eyes.

See, I wanted to be who everybody else *expected* me to be. I wanted to look how everyone else *expected* me to look. I hated myself! I had lived in a box, afraid of exploring who I was born to be. I couldn't face and accept my womanhood because I was cheated—cheated by an old man and a relative who had no business stripping me of my womanhood, my childhood, my rights as a kid, and giving me nothing but childhood traumas. I felt a part of me was robbed and destroyed. Now, I was trying to figure out, *who I am, and* recreating me wasn't the plan or the easiest thing to do when I was left and confused. While redefining myself, I was left with fear, feeling less than, not good enough, not pretty enough,

I'll never forget watching a musical or watching a television show. I couldn't understand why none of the actresses or artists had scars on their bodies, not one. At that time, I didn't know anything about makeup or body makeup. I just thought they were just perfect, even the darker-skinned women were looking like glowing sticks. I started hating myself even more, which I will speak more of in my second book.

The only way I would feel pretty was to hang around prettier popular girls that would recreate me. Maybe they could see the beauty in me and recreate my self-image. I chose the popular kids and chose some of their characteristics to identify with. They would teach me how to dress and tell me to get my hair done more often and wear earrings. I started to take their advice, but still, I didn't feel pretty because my hair was short. I didn't have a dope hairstylist. I had scars on my face, and I had no sense of fashion taste. I started hating being in middle and high school. I became a part of a girl's club called Successful Achievers and attended teen programs, workshops, and events to figure myself out and yet still, I didn't know myself. I grew to hate myself even more because no one noticed me. The little girl inside of me was still trying to figure out the future me because the present me was still struggling with the past me. Everyone around was pretty, except me so I switched it up.

I started hanging with youth that I felt weren't pretty and maybe I would be the one to get hollered at. Sometimes I felt I was being noticed, but I felt I was only noticed because I was fresh meat, not because of my personality or my true beauty. I struggled with myself. I allowed the noise of negative to channel into me and I couldn't kill the noise because I've created it. I became my worst inner-me. The worst thing my dad taught me was to never receive from a man because he will always want something in return. Thanks, Dad, because now, I am a cold, heartless person.

I started to kill the noise and realized I had no voice. Imagine all that you have is bottled up. Everything I had been through was locked up inside, just slowly deteriorating me. Imagine negative thoughts like "Kill yourself," "It's over for you," "If you die, it will all go away," "Make them feel your pain," "You will never make it," and "You're a waste of energy, space, and creation," and "You have no purpose anyway." My mind started to explode, and I had nothing left, but tears, thoughts, and reactions. I had thoughts of wanting to end it all or hurting the world because I had nothing else to give. In my mind, I died a long time ago. However, now my body and spirit were catching up from a place of hurt. Everything in my life was going to BOOM! Then an episode occurred, and the current moment of my life was unfolding, and the timeline of my life was now history. I was trying to live my best life, but I was still stuck in 1999. Silence kills when you are in good standing but lacking financially and do not have enough to keep your life together. I was no longer living paycheck to paycheck. I was living from friends' checks to friends' checks, trying to figure out how to make ends meet.

GEM: As a child, I held resentment against my mother. Because when she was upset, she was skillful with her words that cut deep into your soul. And when she gives you that look, you better RUN!!!! My mom's eyes were like weapons. I used to ignore her calls because I wanted freedom. I became more rebellious when she would leave voice mail thinking I'm with a boy or threatening to lock me out the house because I did not come home after school. That was just the Haitians in her. Overall- my mom is my backbone. She is the sweetness, heart warmth, and loving person I know. I did not understand my mother as a parent and her way of thinking. (Now that I am also a mother of three, I understand) Yes, her word cut like a double sword, but my mother taught me everything she could and did what she can for me to be the woman I am today and to be where I am today. She will give me her last. Yes, she's controlling, as far as, how we move in life, it is only because she loves her children dearly. Do not take this as me bashing my mother, this is coming from a little girl's point of view, who was dealing with hidden hurt and pain and fear of speaking up.

Word of Wisdom: We go through so much in life, not knowing that God is developing us to be something great. We go through long suffering because of the identity God is creating us to be. What do you mean, our past leads us into our purpose in life, into the calling that God has for us. Many of us turned out to be **effective** preachers, teachers, bishops, apostles, prophets and prophetesses, singers, rappers, nurses, actors or actresses, directors, screenwriters, film directors, producers, songwriters, activist, board members, counselors, mentors, coaches, lawyer, doctor, hair stylist, make-up artist, CEO of a nonprofit or for-profit (and the list goes on) - giving birth to that ministry, gift and talent within you. You see I highlighted **effective** because when you are effective, powerful, you can heal those that are hurting, and reach those that need to be reached. I did not know all that I was going through would lead me to be an author, a future preacher/apostle, a counselor, a model, and an advocate for young women, maybe future young men. God makes no mistakes, it is in our pain, we birth something great. Do not take your life, because the enemy knows how powerful you are that is why our thoughts come against us. When the hurdles come your way, when the pressure is on, when you are in the hot heat – just know it is because your blessing is on the way. Something great is about to happen.

Prayer of a helpless person fighting Suicidal Thoughts/Ideation:

Dear Father God,

I am tired. What used am I to this world if I cannot see the reason I am living. Life, man life is just not fair. Learning and striving to stay positive with all that is around me is draining me. I feel useless, worthless, a failure to myself and my family. I feel everything around me just is falling apart. I am trying my best to hold me together. My mind is coming against, I have nowhere to breathe or grasp for air. I feel like I am suffocating. How do I fight when everywhere I turn there are barricades surrounding me? Locked up in one location fighting to get out. This stronghold is holding me tight. My thoughts are telling to just die because peace is what I want. I want to be free from all the things that causing depression. I am following your bible principle. I effortlessly speak life over myself and try so hard to stay positive. What do I DO NOW? I just cannot take it anymore. Do you know what it means to feel lifeless? Why should I live when I am a waste to this earth? What good am I? I don't even see potential in myself. So why should I live again? Why am I here, purpose this purpose that? Okay purpose what? I am having suicidal thoughts again. My thoughts are making me think that I no longer need to live. My thoughts are reminded of all the things, I have experienced and been through. It is also making me believe I serve no purpose on earth, the bills will never get paid, my life is on a thread and there's no way out. My thoughts are reminding me of my past, every hurt and pain, I have endured from being touched, to being taken advantage of, to making me think and feel that I am crazy, the betrayal, feeling insecure, feeling like a failure, my life is worth nothing, I have nothing to offer, I will never be happy or receive happiness, I'll never get married and never enjoy the fullness of life. I am being falsely accused of things, frustration all around me, distractions leading me to death, my situation has people doubting me, I am being overlooked, people downplaying my character, people are setting me out to be a fool, people who say they love and support me are speaking against me and turning their backs on me. My thoughts are telling me it is better to end my life than to live. My thoughts are telling me believable things, it is convincing me and reasoning with me. Making the things I am thinking seems logical. My thoughts are making me think I am not loved. It is making me think it is over, there is no point. I won't make it. It is making me think about all kinds of stuff. I do not have the courage and strength to overcome these thoughts and feelings. God, I am asking for your help. You said if I call on you, your name Jesus. You will answer me. But God when I look at where I am and how far I have come, I can and shall overcome this. When my thoughts begin to speak negatively or remind me of the past, I snap back and tell my thought you are a liar. Yes, I have experienced and gone through that, but I shall live and not die. The enemy is speaking to me so heavily, that I have to remind myself there is something greater and purposeful for me. I thank you for regulating my mind. I speak peace over my mind. For you said in your word be anxious for nothing and peace you will give me. You said you gave me the spirit of love and a sound mind. You said for you know the plans you have concerning me. You said you will keep me in perfect peace if my mind stayed on you. God, I am asking for peace of mind today. I shall not have suicidal thoughts. When the thoughts of fear, failure, destruction, doubts, unworthy, unloved- when those spirits come over me. Remind me of your love, your grace, your blood you shed on Calvary. Just for me. Remind me of all those hurdles I have overcome during my years on earth. Remind me that you never failed me and never will. For when my father and mother forsake me. You will not. Remind me of the love you have for me. Your daily bread.

In Jesus' Name. Amen.

Side Note: If you ever feel that way, please call someone, the national suicide hotline 800-273-8255, or seek counseling immediately or contact a local mobile crises. DO NOT, handle this alone. The rate of suicide increases daily. YOU DO MATTER... A safety plan will be in place. You are not a failure. You are worthy. You are loved and it will not bring you peace spiritually or peace to others knowing there is someone who cares. Do not walk this walk alone. Think about this, after you take your life then what? PEACE ?! There's no peace because there's questions that are unanswered wondering how we or someone could have supported or help you to live a better or peace life. You think it will bring peace, but others will suffer grieving over you. You may feel helpless, hopeless, useless, like a failure, unworthy, unloved, unwanted, unfulfilling, a waste, pointless, undeserving, annoyed, shameless, guilty. All these things and more. The bottom line is you are not that. You are far more than that. There is someone who wants you, need you, loves you, cares about you, want to hear and share your pain, care enough to want to help you get your life in order. Everything of the past is damaging but you have so many years to make it better, to heal, to fight through to help someone else get through. You may want out – want to end it all. Every day is a new day to START ALL OVER AGAIN. God GRACED is sufficient and is enough to give us chances to live an abundant-meaningful life. RESET, RESTART, RECHARGE. I love you!!!!!

For those who have loss someone through suicide and you did all you can. I want to say I love you; you did all you can to say them. You did what you can to help them live. Sometimes life can be too much that what we go through we feel that a better way is OUT. When that is not the answer, but PEACE is what they want and need. PEACE from all they have experienced, genuine LOVE, and to be UNDERSTOOD. An ear to hear and a heart to love. Showing up and being there is what they need. Your presences. Thank you for doing all that you could. Rest, pray, and be at peace. I pray peace, comfort, and a fresh of wind to fall upon you, for God to breathe life into you, and for grace to be your portion.

PRESENT SELF

Dear Present Self,

I am sorry you had to experience such trauma and had no one to talk to or support you during the times like those. I know it robbed you of your childhood and your sexuality. The experiences caused you to have trust issues, and suffer from self-rejection which caused low self-esteem and self-hatred and caused you to grow up as a shy child. It also caused you to feel less than and feel that it was okay to be touched sexually, even when you knew the feeling was wrong. It also caused you not to be able to explore your identity as a woman and enjoy your sexual desires with your future spouse. I'm sorry you've felt alone. I'm sorry you felt no one cared or that you were the only one to experience this. I'm sorry you did not seek counseling to overcome the trauma.

Nevertheless, I want to extend my heart to you and say you grew up to be a beautiful woman, a phenomenal woman, a great friend, a motivator with great potential, and someone others can talk to and look up to. You turned out to be God's greatest gift to earth. You are a miracle and a blessing. You will heal other women by your testimony. I extend my heart to all the women and men who've been touched by a relative, a close family member, a friend of the family, or by your parent. They left you lonely and didn't try to support you to overcome the traumatic experience or protect you. I extend my heart to you. I know you questioned why they didn't believe you, why did they touch me?

I'm pretty sure their answer was they were scared, or they had to do what they had to, or they would blame you for it instead of realizing you didn't ask for it. Your parents probably had been through what you been through and didn't know how to advocate for you. I know that's a weak excuse because now you are suffering from post-traumatic stress syndrome (PTSD). Some of you may or may not know this, but you suffered or are suffering from impulsive disorder or anxiety or depression or mania all because of your childhood traumas that could have been avoided or could have been treated by a great therapist. I know how it feels to grow up having to guard your heart and deal with trust issues, be mad at the world, and walk around with an attitude of thinking everyone is your enemy. People don't understand that a lot of your character comes from your childhood experiences. During those stages, your parents didn't understand that these memories and experiences would become a part of you and create a new identity for you. I'm sorry that your parents didn't believe anything you said or stated that you were overly dramatic, overreacting, lying, making things up, or seeking attention, not knowing that alone would cause you to be enraged, to live in unforgiveness, to have self-hatred, to run away from home, or to want to commit suicide. They ignored the real situation.

I am sorry for your parents. I am sorry for your parents because the situations created something great within you that is a *strong mother lover* that can knock down *giants* or any obstacles that come your way. *You* are like the caterpillar that turns into a butterfly or a tree that goes through many storms, but still manages to stand strong. That is who you are. You are great and have a great future waiting for you. Don't let the past kill your future for your future has what you always dreamed about. Learn to forgive and let God heal the right way for a better relationship with people and for a change in character and how you respond to others.

THE VOICE

Your voice is a powerful tool. Your voice is what helps you to speak and express yourself. It is a way of communication, it is a sound, it is a network, it is healing, it is a tone, it is passion, it is a platform, it is self-confidence; it is a story. Your voice overshadows things, even pain. Your voice is what people die for. It's what puts political and non-political people in their stances. Malcolm X, Dr. Martin Luther King, Tu-Pac, Biggie, Dr. Sebi, Nipsey Hussle, and many other legends' voices created their platforms to enable us to move forward. Our voices are legendary.

Voices carry out a sound wave that one can listen to. It's just unique and strong to know that your voice counts too. It is your voice that will attract those who are silent to speak. People will try to mute you and have you suffer in silence due to their past silence or the pain they suffered in silence. Someone else's voice should not downplay yours. Remember this, what happens in the dark always comes to light when you know what you are fighting for and why. It may be intimidating or aggressive, but when you become powerful, your voice stands out.

My voice is different for a reason, the same reason why I speak differently. We all don't sound the same. Some speak aggressively, passively, or assertively. Our tones range from high to low, but that should not take away from who we are and what we stand for.

Many times, we are scared to speak because we question whether we will say the right things, or fear what the reaction of someone else will be when we speak. Will we hurt their feelings? Will they read into what I say too deeply? Do they even care? Am I saying the right thing? At some point, they will. It is okay to think about your audience and how you want to present what you want to say. An authentic relationship does not give room for fakeness. A strong foundation doesn't have room for cracks. Here's another way to look at it. When rappers write their lyrics, they don't worry about whether the lyrics are offensive or not. They make their point; there is no filter in their songs. Guess what? We still sing the songs. Whether we agree to disagree, if the beat is right and the bars are tough, we forget the deeper meaning of it. And that doesn't stop their money from flowing in. Know your audience and speak their language. Our voice is what sets us free from the mental slave. Don't let our emotions take over to the point it affects us either long term or short term. At times, some things are meant to be brushed off, but some things are not. If the situation carries through your day and you continue to meditate on it day and night, it is affecting you. You need to find a healthy way to come to peace with it. If not, toss it- trash it, and do not go back to it.

It's important to have your voice and to mute others' voices. Being muted not only affects who you are but affect your ability to navigate your own life without the voices of others dictating your decisions. This is how you will be available to develop to know who you are and what you stand for. The voices of others will cause you to abort how you feel and make decisions that will affect you either long term or short term. It depends on who you allow whispering in your ears, who you allow to be your voice outside of yours. The wrong voices will cause you to abort your destination and bury your pain in areas you have no business burying. Don't allow individuals to steal your voice. It's alright to tune out those voices because those voices create barriers preventing you from making the right decisions for yourself.

Your voice is powerful; it is effective. When you're not walking in that authority, you lose power. Your voice is your authority. It provides statements as to who you are, and your actions reinforce your integrity. You must take ownership of your voice. Be first and careful so you can hear yourself properly without the voices of others. Stay true to who you are. Don't self-sabotage your inner voice because that inner voice is telling you to do the right thing. Trust your inner voice. Don't adjust your voice to make someone feel comfortable.

To women, our voices are like flowers, ready to blossom. At times it won't be. I don't want to make women's voices a chanting song or a chatter of voices. Speak when needed with some integrity and assertiveness. Don't be too passive but give that space where anyone can come to you and speak. The point is for women to speak up when needed, not to be silenced. We carry so much rage when we bottle things inside, then we become categorized as crazy— the crazy woman that did this, the crazy woman that did that or said this. Air it out with moderation! The truth hurts. It hurts because of the reality of it. We don't want to accept or face what's really going on. When we do, we become more hurt. The truth is the truth should make you a better individual and mold your character to become a better you. It will set you free.

I'm at a point in my life where I want to change what's around me to grow in a better light. I once was someone beautiful and now I've blossomed into someone phenomenal. Love yourself enough to give yourself attitude and the courage to move forward and live. Love yourself enough to find the value you have within yourself. Love yourself enough to gain self-respect. Nothing or no one can change that. Be loyal to yourself first and always have and show gratitude.

As for men, man will be a man. He will only feel safe and secure when the woman of his life makes him feel that way. If you mess up, make it right. Don't focus on what's wrong; focus on what's right. Some men need an indication that he is doing right, and some need validation. Be grateful for what you have because tomorrow is not promised. Yes, men want their cake and eat it too. Women, we need to stop coming into the relationship with expectations of your spouse or the relationship; the same goes for men too. Don't be anybody's door mat even when it's not intentional. Be grateful for what you have because someone else is wishing for it or lurking for it or chasing for it or plotting on it. Once the door is cracked open, she will slip their way through. You'll miss out on what you once had. What God has ordained for you, is for you, *no matter what*! Be kind, give love, and give what you would want someone to give you.

LOVE: FORGIVENESS, RECONNECTING, RESTORING

"When you need to be loved, you take love wherever you can find it. When you are desperate to be loved, feel love, know love, you seek out what you think love should look like. When you find love, or what you think love is, you will lie, kill, and steal to keep it. But learning about real love comes from within. It cannot be given. It cannot be taken away. It grows from your ability to re-create within yourself, the essence of loving experiences you have had in your life."

-Iyanla Vanzant (Quote by Iyanla Vanzant: "When you need to be loved, you take love wherever..." (goodreads.com)

Love is being able to love yourself enough that no one can make you feel unwanted. Love is making yourself happy before making someone else happy. Love is being loyal to yourself, first, before being loyal to someone else. Love is being able to make peace with your past to make peace with your present and future. Love is forgiving what happened and moving forward to something better and or new. Love is conquering self to conquer someone else. Reconnecting love is the best happily ever after. The "I miss you and I love you," the "I want you back and need you" type of reconnections. The make-up connection of loss of time. Forgiving the past, leaving the old, and starting new. Reconnecting love is healthy without being platonic. The feeling of holding hands once again and sharing happy moments. It's never too late to reconnect and start over from where you first met or where you left off. If you are in a healthy space, creating a healthy moment and you are at peace. Love is never too late to give. Love will have you singing harmony, your heart will beat without skipping a beat. Love will have you smiling from ear to ear.

Reconnected love creates memories and stronger vibrations for each other. To feel this feeling, you first must love yourself enough to give love. Respect yourself enough to respect others. Love doesn't have to be for a spouse; it can be for family, relatives, friends, enemies, strangers, etc. Reconnecting love comes from taking time apart from each other. From being able to say alright we need space to focus on self again to love, nurture, and care for an individual. Taking time apart means time for reconstructing yourself, recovering from the past, and loving yourself, which is truly important. It means being happy where you are and where you are going and being able to accept the love that is being poured into you. You want to flourish first within the self, to outpour that same loving spirit into someone else. You want the love to be so fresh that after a long time, the love turns into "I miss you; I love you." That's reconnecting.

Allow time and space to create a moment for yourself to start over or to process through what it is that you want. There can be a lesson to learn from and to help you move on to what you want or searching for. Not only will time apart benefit your relationship but give you a bonus to add to the next relationship. Reconnecting is a beautiful thing. It allows you to love *again*. Love is a beautiful thing. It has its definition. You can define love. Everyone has their definition of love and it's alright to not know right away what it is. Taking time apart will help you learn what love is. Knowing your worth will help you know what love is, so you don't tolerate bullshit. What you bring to the table will help you learn what love is. Many factors come into play that will teach, show, and provide examples of what healthy love is or looks like. A man or a woman can teach, show, or provide what love is or what it looks like.

When you can identify love, reconnecting with your partner or spouse will be a beautiful thing. It will be love at first sight. You can let go of the past, forgive, and move on. Take it slow. Remember, things that come easily, you lose quickly while things that come through the mud, challenges, and trials are cherished more. When you fight for a relationship or when a relationship is from a teaching standpoint, you have a lot to work with. There are a lot of cuts and paste or copies here and there. Taking advice only applies if it works for you. Taking advice only works if it applies to *you*. For example, everyone's character only speaks to certain audiences. Cardi B's attitude has a specific audience. Does it mean she has to change to fit everyone? No. If she is authentic, she will draw those she needs to draw. That's how love works. Don't change to accommodate; only if needed. Not everything a person says will fit your agenda of how to make a relationship work. You can take some things and, if everything someone says works for you, then it does. For example, I love how Jada Pinkett Smith and Will Smit spoke on the Red Table Talk about how taking a time apart helped build their relationship, about how they didn't take what society, people, or social media defined what marriage is or what it looks like and let that interfere with their definition or views of marriage. They, together, decided to define it in their own term by deconstructing and applying what works for them. The keywords are *"works for them."* Not everyone will understand, accept, or value your decision because it's not "traditional "or that's not what it is. What works for you, works for you.

As stated before, reconnecting with love is a beautiful thing—the feeling of being loved again while taking it slow to trust again. It doesn't have to mean moving back together again or maybe it does. It's your level and definition of where you want it to be but allow space and time to develop the "I miss you and I love you. I want to see you" while still having time and space for yourself.

Take time to understand each other and think about if the shoe was on the other foot. Women speak about emotion better than men. Men, stop speaking in the logical sense; express yourselves in the emotional sense. Express your heart, men. Women, hold men accountable for their actions but show emotions as well to work towards their hurt. It's not acceptable for men or women to make excuses for why they act the way they act. If you're not growing, you are dying. Growth is important within yourself or in a relationship whether it is with a spouse, family members, friends, loved ones, or on the job. Pray for the present situation. Communicate the problem. Identify the problem or issue, call it out, and approach it. Men, be open to feedback and acknowledge it's a needed practice to grow. Understand, ladies, when a person speaks based upon their past, don't just accept it. Help them through it. Don't let a person fail when they put themselves out there. Sometimes the best method is to let the person fail, so pull back. Don't tolerate things that don't make you happy.

To reconnect and love again is to love yourself first. After you love yourself, go to the root of the problem, meaning; make peace with your past and accept your past for what it is. Look at your past and turn it into good. Look at it as a blessing and not a curse. Everything in life can be viewed both as good and bad. When you can be at peace with your past and come to the realization of where the misconnection happened, then you can build. Love overpowers everything. "But now faith, hope, and love remain—these three. The greatest of these is love." (1 Corinthians 13:13 WEB).

NO MORE

"Release and detach from every person, every circumstance, every condition, and every situation that no longer serves a divine purpose in your life. All things have a season, and all seasons must come to an end. Choose a new season, filled with purposeful thoughts and activities."

— Iyanla Vanzant

"Breaking that cycle that no longer serves you or your procreation any purpose. Breaking the family cycle, generational cycle, cycle within yourself, cycles that you attracted to your life or brought to your life. No more cycling pain and hurt. No more repeating family systems, mental issues, attributes, upbringings, etc. Break those cycles of bondage and battles."

– Cassandra Edouard

This is for individuals who have been silent for a long time, the ones who felt they did not have a voice. Whether it was from being silent to thoughts, silent to man, silent to other people, silent to him, silent to her, or silent to the world. No man, no one, or thing should cause you to bury that powerful voice. I mean nothing should ever silence you. No problem should silence you to depression, anxiety, or misleading behavior. You are strong enough to voice what is unheard. We have been silenced for too long, way too long, since ancient times. We should not let our voice be powerless, ignored, criticized, mocked, invalidated, or indicted. Do not let words choke you and thoughts crumble you. Do not let your mind control you;

you control it. We lived in our minds for too long and do not open our mouths or use our voices. We have been silent for too long to not release the gifts inside of us. We can use our mouths to curse and speak negatively, but we cannot use our mouths to speak the promises or hidden gifts within us.

All we would do is create and release bitterness, negative thoughts and actions, suicidal thoughts, revenge, rage, sickness, and resentment. Instead, roar! Roar louder, but never destroy. Roar in silent movement like a cheetah coming for his prey. Find it within yourself to shake what's unshaken, move the unmovable and break the unbreakable with that powerful voice. No more blaming people for your wrongdoings or theirs. Accept the wrongs and the right you have done. Take ownership and free yourselves, your spirit, and your mind. Do not let the stigma of mental health eliminate you from getting the help or services that are needed. Mental health is healthy for the mind, body, and spirit. When the mind is healthy, the soul will become and can be free. Free the mind for a renewal of spirit. Mental health does not mean you have a mental illness, a disorder, or issues although it can lead to mental disorders or illnesses. But to prevent that, we need to be in a healthy place.

Mental health means our minds need to be free, free from the emotional and mental bondage of thoughts. Therefore, we need to create a new way of thinking and set healthy conditions for positive thinking and for cleansing of the soul. When we are not thinking positively, it causes a battle of the mind. The battle of the mind causes our thoughts to become unstable and leads us into unclear thoughts. We now become criminals in our minds and enemies with our thoughts because we are too busy functioning on a negative level. This then creates death to our bodies and our spirit, which kills off brain cells and develops diseases or illnesses in our bodies that are or are not, curable. So, let's free our mental state for a healthy mindset.

From now on, when you think of mental health, think of the well-being of the mind. We need our minds to be at peace and aligned for our body and spirit to respond accordingly. Stand up for your mental health. No more suicidal thoughts, no more battles of the mind, no more challenges, no more drunkenness, no more bottling up or swallowing up your problems and dreams. Let's be stress-free. Self-care is very important. Your well-being is important. Let's release those skeletons in our closet for better closure, self-healing, and for a better future. If you're looking for a support system or guidance, find a supportive organization or groups or create such a group, write, find a new hobby, travel, or do something outside of sitting in a box with depression or drunkenness. Release and try to confide in someone—stranger, counselor, pastor, family, relative, friend, or homeless person.

Words of advice and for the respect of self and others: if someone confided in you, please do not burn bridges by exposing someone else's life challenges, issues, problems, circumstances, or crises. There must be *no* judgment because we all have skeletons in our closets that we brushed under the rug. According to the Bible, no sin is greater than another. No one has walked a perfect line. We all fall short, even the newborn. To the counselors out there, if you are not passionate about helping your clients heal, *please* leave the field. This field is about advocating for those who can't advocate for themselves and those who need healing from their past. They don't need selfish people who don't care about their problems. Stop doing more damage to their life. My professor, Dr. Owens, once told me, "Don't go out damaging your clients more than they are already. Do some soul searching, sit with the situation, do some research, teach your client to do better and understand them and help them." It is imperative to become an effective counselor.

You are a counselor for a reason, not to play with the individual's feelings and take their money for pleasure. Yes, counselors need to make a living, but your people's brokenness is not for sale or a display. They have to deal with that daily with the justice system, in their personal lives, at their workplace, churches, businesses, anywhere and everywhere, and with the government behind the scenes. You wouldn't like it if a person played and monopolized your life and gambled with it. *Do not do it to the clients.* Loyalty is best. Practice that. There is a reason why they came to you—trust. If you know you cannot build that trust and listen, let them know and let them go. People need healing and the only way that can happen is if humanity can come together and help heal each other. We are a powerful force and together we can help each other heal. The answers are not just within us, but in someone else as well. So, let's be each other's treatment, coping mechanism, and strength. This message goes to the church leaders, random leaders, and anyone with a title or without.

Today, I blame **FEAR**. The fear of the unknown. Fear if you speak, this will be the cause of the reaction. Fear is the reason we all have been crippled, scarred, bitter, content, scared, and living in bondage. Fear of being misunderstood, mishandled, mistreated, rejected, abandon, hurt, living in pain, losing someone or something, fear of injustice, fear to strike back, fear of walking away from a relationship, friendship, work environment, business deals, family members, self, anything, and anyone or places that no longer served a great purpose in our lives. Fear of being delivered or healed. **Fear of letting go** or moving on. Just FEAR-ing. Fear will cause you to miss the vision God has for you, the plan, the insight, the instructions, the manual to the next chapter of your life.

I did not realize how much fear kept me in bondage, and held me back from seeing my full potential, the master plan from my Creator, God. It caused my setback and settling for people, places, things, and opportunities that I am overqualified for or do not deserve nor shouldn't have invested my time. I even caused my setback and missed out on many opportunities due to talking myself out of great things. Because I failed to see beyond the fear.

Fear will cause you to be stuck in a situation that God wants to deliver us from, but we kept going back or are scared to move forward. So, we allow fear to silence us, cripple us, and keep us muted on things that can lead to stress, anxiety, depression, suicidal thoughts, and then suicide. Fear will have us respond negatively, behave negatively, and be ready to fight whomever, quick with the mouth. Fear will have you reasoning instead of responding from a logical place. FEAR. It will have you in doubt, in your emotions, in distress, in panic mode, in suspicion, paranoid, worrying, uneasy, misunderstood, nervous, thinking people, place, or things are a threat to you or for you, cause pain, put you in a dangerous place (mentally, emotionally, physically, psychologically, financially). Fear is lethal, a deadly weapon, evil. We do things or say things out of **FEAR**.

Something I have learned is that "For God didn't give us a **spirit of fear, but of power, love, and self-control."** (2 Timothy 1:7 **WEB).** What I love so much about this scripture is that we all need a sound mind, the battle is in our minds. When we realize that we have the power to break fear, we can walk in love within ourselves, and with others, and not fear anything that comes our way because we will have the spirit of wisdom and good counsel. The way only for us to receive and see it- if we submit to God and allow him to have his way within us, in our hearts. The very place he wants to be. Then you will see a change. If we abide (draw onto him) in God, he will cause us to be fruitful - meaning he will heal us, deliver us from ourselves, break cycles, give us our heart desires, peace, joy, the husband, the wife, the career, your identity, your purpose, the promises he spoke over your life, the finance, the wealth, the resources, and the connections- divine connection. You get the point.

Remember, God wants you to have life and life more abundantly. He wants to preserve us for his calling and his purpose. We have so much to offer and give, so much love hidden within us. If we stay stuck in fear, in that wilderness place, that Egypt he talks about. We will be like the Israelites; never making it to the promised land or taking years to get into that promised land that God promise and gave our forefather Abraham. We must first heal from our past, remove the spirit of fear, and LIVE, LOVE, and LAUGH.

SO... Let's declare.... **I DECLARE:** No more tears. No more hurt people hurt people. No more cycling pain. No more hurt me. No more trauma. No more games. No more having people in your circle who don't want to see you sore like an eagle. No more feelings of being rejected or obligated. No more self-doubt. No more fear. No more low self-esteem. No more playing the fool. No more tolerating disrespected. No more giving your all to something or someone who seems not to appreciate, love, value or give back the same energy being put in. No more losing yourself to please others. No more putting your health on the line. No more broken heart. No more suffering silence. No more searching for and accepting convenient love. No more self-abuse or being abuse. No more living in unforgiveness. NO MORE!!!! No more trying to prove people wrong or right. No more toxicity. No more having people dim your light. No more tolerating bullshit, lies, deceitful spirits, conniving spirits, people, or things that don't represent or reflect who you are. NO MORE!! No more carrying death weight. No more soul ties. No more living in the past. No more tolerating and giving in to foolery and mockery. No more drama. NO MORE. No more foolish acts; be *wise*!!! No more damaging hearts, spirits, and souls. No more operating in confusion, infliction, and affliction. NO MORE!!

Love yourself and appreciate you enough that no one or nothing can stand in your way or stop you or put you down. If loving yourself means seeking counseling, make that first step of researching someone you can seek guidance from, true guidance. Make sure the person has been counseling for more than ten years. If the person has not been counseling for ten years or more, then make sure the person knows their craft, is dedicated and motivated, and is true to their work. It will give you perfect peace with yourself and healing will take place. A piece of advice for those in a relationship or trying to build a foundation with someone: if an individual can disrespect you in front of your family or friends and call you all types of disrespectful names, the individual doesn't respect or love you. The individual doesn't deserve your love, your presence, your wholeness, your newness. Love yourself enough to never let an individual belittle you no matter who it is. Hold yourself up high.

Keep your integrity; it will take you a long way. It will be hard to love someone who mistreats you because you won't look at that person the same way. All the person will do is guide you into bitterness and give you a sorrowful heart, helping you create a bigger wall that doesn't need to be there. Never allow an individual to manipulate you and put you last because of his or her insecurities. Don't let him or her make you feel like second place. Don't let him or her make you feel as if he or she leaves you, you should chase them. NO! Let him or her leave. If another woman or man is in his or her best interest, let them be together. Let him or her be while you get yourself together. If he or she was meant for you, they'll come back into your life. If not, you have someone better, who you can count on and who is waiting to cherish you, love you, smile with you, cry with you, dance with you, build with you, build you up, clean you up, pray with you, educate you, and love your flaws and turn them into something positive. Lastly, he or she will flourish with you. He or she will be able to create a strong foundation during the storm. A strong foundation is *never broken;* it stands strong and firm. In a relationship built on a strong foundation, the couple takes every attack together no matter the circumstances or situations. Sometimes, to build a foundation, the foundation must be broken and reconstructed so it won't be easily broken. Picture your relationship as a tree, deeply rooted that no storms can move it.

Quick GEM: People make temporary decisions based on emotions, which causes or destroys long-term situations or cancels short-term circumstances. So much will be thrown at you to distract you and make you end your life. Don't pay attention to what's around you. Be strong enough to stand still and say, "Thank you." Acknowledging the good and the bad so no matter what is being presented in front of me, you can manage it and won't give it too much power to destroy you. Life is like a season—everything is temporary. Even when the season changes and it is winter, it doesn't change the fact that spring will still come.

To my women: We, as women, have been through so many life challenges since slavery and ancient times. It is time to be delivered. Oftentimes, we think if we stay in a toxic relationship or come across life challenges or crises, the only way out is to commit suicide or live in a lie. That's not true. There's more to life than what you see or what you face. So, no more making excuses for other actions or blaming yourself for what they have done. There's a point in life where karma shall come upon their life and destroy what they thought would destroy you. Also, we must stop playing the victim because of something we created with our own hands. When we decide to face our karma, deal with it, clean it up, and start over; *we must be honest with yourself first.*

The best thing you can ever do is make peace within yourself to give peace to someone else. This is in any relationship you have with people no matter who they are. Karma presents itself differently, but it will come around, no matter how long it takes. It shall pop up in your life for any wrongs you have done in your life. *Be very careful* moving forward. Forgive, heal, and move forward. It is important to heal from the past hurt, acknowledge it, and say thank you. If you have a great man at home, love him, cherish him, and put him first. A man deserves happiness, especially when he has the weight of the world on his shoulders. Even if it's the smallest thing you can do, make it count. He will cherish it. Our men work hard to make sure they put a smile on our faces. There's nothing wrong with running his bubble baths and vice versa. There's nothing wrong with saying, "Bae, I'll treat tonight." Our men need attention, someone to hear them when they cry, someone to rub their feet and kiss them good night. You may not be his homeboy, but he'll sure be able to speak to you as one. He will come to you and honestly speak the truth without having to sugarcoat a thing.

Be more supportive to your man and speak positively to him, need him, praise him, show interest, lovingly correct him, challenge him by inspiring him, expose him to greatness, do greater things than he, and pray for and with him. A woman is supposed to be the man's peace of mind, his stress reliever. A lot of people won't agree with this one. When I say become his peace of mind, I mean to give him what the streets can't or what the world can't. No stress, no fights, and no frustrations; complain less. If he goes out of his way for you and puts you first before his mother and family, he loves you.

To all my men, men are too silent. No one can hear them because their silence has been dimmed. No one wants to hear their pain or comfort their cry. The heavy burden they have carried since slavery is killing their pride. We all, as a Black race, have been silenced. The world has been silent. The churches have been silent. Silence is a deadly weapon no matter what you are going through in life, no matter what challenges. We all are desensitized human beings, just walking around spreading unhealthy love and negativity. We are just polluting the air. Let's reconnect and spread love.

As women, we are passive, submissive, assertive, passionate, caring, loving, strong-minded, and guarded for a reason. There's a time to be these things. There's a time to pull out those character cards and say, "Hey, I'm not tolerating this" and there's a time to say, "Bae, I love you. Bae, come meet me in the bedroom." I'm sure he'll get super excited. If you're used to raising your voice, try being a little passive and talk in a different tone because that matters as well. If you're used to complaining, change it; don't rationalize things or jump to conclusions. If you have tried all these and you see no results, he was not meant for you. God didn't ordain him for your life. Throw him away. You will not benefit from him, especially if he doesn't bring anything to the table, but his two cents for entertainment.

Whatever your struggle is, you will finish strong, and you shall finish strong. Keep pushing. Speak what you want or desire into existence. Send positive vibrations into the atmosphere. Tell the universe or God what you are looking for. Forgive yourself and others for what they have done in the past. Tell yourself, "I'm coming out." No more sorrow, no pain. I am free. Free from heartache, free from troubles, free from doubt, free from low self-esteem, free from the opinions of others, free from my enemies, free from my adversaries, free from negative energy, free from negative thoughts, free from my mind, free from bondage, free from depression, free from the societal definition of me or happiness, free from the world.

BE Free!!!! Free from everything that you feel is holding you back. *Love you first, pour into yourself first then love others with an open heart. No more* holding onto what others have done. *No more* tolerating what you don't want in your life or space. NO MORE. Let's make a vow *never* to operate in *hurt* or *pain. Never let the troubles of others, cause pain in your life.* Make a vow never to be silent again, to never let the voices in your head cause you to attempt to take your life or rob you of your happiness, peace, and joy. Or let the voices devalue your character or make you settle for less. Vow to never let a man's voice overpower yours concerning *yourself, your value, or your morality.* Vow to be the ideal woman you imagine yourself to be, who God called and created you to be, *and not what society or social media says it is or what you see in someone else.* I vow. You vow. We vow together. We will no longer let FEAR cripple us anymore. Remember God loves you, no matter the state you are in. Be who God says you are, not what man (people) says you are. This goes for me too. Remember this: What God has for you it is for you. No matter what it is, who it is, if God says it is yours, believe it is yours. You won't have to fight for it, compete for it, to stress about it. Whether, it is a man, a woman, a position, a title, a business, a home, the desired salary, or whatever your heart desire.

Lastly, if you are going through hell, I mean, everything is going and coming against you, know there's a blessing attached to that attack. You are also being tested for that blessing. Whether it is an upgrade, a promotion, or whatever it is. The enemy knows when you are about to elevate. The enemy can be spiritual and natural – meaning a person. When people see you are about to be blessed, they send something or become that distraction or frustration to cause you to lose focus on that goal. Be careful of people, who are jealous of you or want to be you, they will do everything in their power to keep you stuck, in lack, in bondage, not to move into our destiny. IF YOU PRAY and have God on your side. Now that you will and shall WIN. You already have the VICTORY. I am a living witness. So, keep pushing and apply pressure.

Acknowledgments

I thank God for giving me the wisdom and knowledge to put this book together. The words to say and for allowing me to go through my life experiences and be creative to write this book to help someone like myself find inner healing and be the voice to the voiceless. I would like to thank my children, Ava, Jeremiah, and Mikal for being such a motivation to me and making me feel like a great mother even when I feel like I am not the best. You guys showed me and taught me to be nothing but the best and to give the best. Thank you, Jeremiah and Mikal, for drying my tears when I cry, telling me you love me and having me watch what I say. Thank you for giving me a reason to smile when I feel as if I have nothing to smile about, and for speaking life into my life. Thank you, Ava, for giving me the confidence that unable to see within myself. Thank you for giving me the strength and peace I needed to flourish within. I believe this book will teach you guys to be a voice and not to be silenced, to stay true and loyal to yourself, to seek God first, and be great leaders to the nations and not let anyone give you an identity. Value yourself more than anything. Also, take ownership of your own actions and your past.

I would like to also thank my parents for instilling morals and values in me, for teaching me spiritual teachings, for creating me, for not giving up on me, and for always being my biggest fan and supporter no matter what I went through. Thank you for allowing me to grow and develop into a strong and phenomenal woman. A special thanks to my siblings for being such a motivation for me and allowing me to make mistakes and seeing my growth. Although never judging, they were hard on me because they saw growth and potential in me that I didn't. I would like to thank myself for allowing me to grow through so much pain to find my strength, peace, and healing. I thank myself for being strong enough to shine through the pain even when I did not want to take responsibility, but I did. I am grateful I was aware of my mistakes and willing to humble myself to make a change and be able to receive counsel for a better future.

To my hurt and pain, thank you for teaching me no pain no gain. You have to lose to win again. Thank you for allowing me to grow through this journey to heal to learn who I am in order to earn me and to be love and to love the right way. So I can love the man God has ordained for me- to go after what I truly deserve, a healthy relationship, Godly love, peace, and happiness within. Thank you for what we've been through together because it drew me closer to God. Thank you for feeding me the wisdom and knowledge to become a wealthy woman for my family. Thank you for choosing me to be the mother to our children and an amazing future wife for my God-ordained husband. I Thank God for allowing what He allowed just so I can be where I am today.

I can't forget my loved ones, for understanding while I was going through my journey. Some of you may not understand and it was not meant for you to understand because it was my storm to go through to blossom the way I did. I love you all. A special thanks in advance to all my readers for investing in yourself and in me. Thank you for allowing me to be creative and use this platform to share our stories. Remember God does not make mistakes. He allows you to go through the process to develop, shape, and mold a new you. Casting all your worries on him, because he cares for you. Peter 5: 7, and he will make your paths straight. Proverbs 3: 5-6.

Some inspiring words from the legendary Nipsey Hussle, "Find your purpose, go get it, and grind. Design yourself. You can have it all, it's all about your reason. Speak something into the universe. Don't waste your time. Take control of things. Don't live basic. Live your life and grow. You will be passing through stages of life, going through ups and downs. Fly like an eagle. You have nothing to lose. Self-educate and play chess. Pace yourself. Fight them demons. Keep the devil in his hole and shine a light on people. You have souls to save. Hussle and Motivate. Your circle will get smaller because everybody can't go. Make sure the ones you have around stick to the script, that's written in stone to make your dreams come true. It takes dedication, hard work plus patience, and sacrifices to be a voice, a legendary, and self-made. Just never let a hard time humble us. BOSS UP, Re-Invent. Don't waste air." (These words came from his inspiring songs: Double Up, Dedication, Victory Lap, Real Big, Hussle & Motivate, Right Hand to God, Last Time That I Checc'd, Grinding all My Life, Blue Laces 2, and Racks in The Middle.)